Comings and Goings

Text copyright © Gordon Giles 2015
The author asserts the moral right to be identified as the author of this work

Published by
The Bible Reading Fellowship
15 The Chambers, Vineyard
Abingdon OX14 3FE
United Kingdom
Tel: +44 (0)1865 319700
Email: enquiries@brf.org.uk
Website: www.brf.org.uk
BRF is a Registered Charity

ISBN 978 0 85746 376 0

First published 2015
10 9 8 7 6 5 4 3 2 1 0
All rights reserved

Acknowledgements
Unless otherwise stated, scripture quotations are taken from The New Revised
Standard Version of the Bible, Anglicised edition, copyright © 1989, 1995 by the
Division of Christian Education of the National Council of the Churches of Christ
in the United States of America. Used by permission. All rights reserved.

Extracts from the Authorised Version of the Bible (The King James Bible), the
rights in which are vested in the Crown, are reproduced by permission of the
Crown's Patentee, Cambridge University Press.

Scripture quotations from The Revised Standard Version of the Bible, copyright ©
1946, 1952, 1971 by the Division of Christian Education of the National Council
of the Churches of Christ in the United States of America. Used by permission. All
rights reserved.

Extracts from 'When I needed a neighbour' by Sydney Carter. © 1965 Stainer &
Bell Ltd, London, England. www.stainer.co.uk. Used by permission.

'Now is eternal life' by G.W. Briggs (1875–1959). Verse reproduced by permission
of Oxford University Press. All rights reserved.

'His Father's house he enters in' by George Timms. © The English Hymnal
Company. Used by permission.

'O West Bank town of Bethlehem' copyright © Martin Leckebusch. Used by kind
permission of Martin Leckebusch.

'Lord of the boundless curves of space' by Albert F. Bayly (1901–84). © 1988
Oxford University Press. Verse reproduced by permission. All rights reserved.

Cover photo: Pearl/Lightstock

Every effort has been made to trace and contact copyright owners for material
used in this resource. We apologise for any inadvertent omissions or errors, and
would ask those concerned to contact us so that full acknowledgement can be
made in the future.

A catalogue record for this book is available from the British Library
Printed and bound by CPI Group (UK) Ltd, Croydon CR0 4YY

Comings and Goings

Retracing the Christmas story through place and time

Gordon Giles

Acknowledgements

No book is ever a single-hearted effort. This book has its roots in the Holy Land itself and I am immensely grateful for the opportunities to visit Israel, Jordan and Egypt with groups over the last decade or so. I have travelled with the curates in the Edmonton Episcopal Area of London and learned from them, and I have travelled with my parishioners of St Mary Magdalene's in Enfield. I am indebted to Alistair McCabe, Andy Webster and Rosemary Nutt of McCabe Travel, and Geoff and Ann Crago who have made so much possible, and to all my fellow pilgrims for their insights, their patience and their enthusiasm. I am particularly grateful to the Revd Stephen Leader, my colleague in Post-Ordination Training, to Canon Philip Spence and to Bishop Peter Wheatley, whose retirement as Bishop of Edmonton fell on the very day I completed the manuscript. This book is a thank-you gift to them.

Contents

Introduction

On the gravestone of the poet T.S. Eliot (1888–1965) is a brief quotation that sums up a great deal of his poetic thinking: 'In my beginning is my end... in my end is my beginning'. So on this Advent journey we begin at the end. I invite you to travel with me backwards in time, starting at the end, as T.S. Eliot might put it, and arriving as we conclude at the very beginning of all things. This shall be but one strand of our journey—one of the two rails on which we ride, a temporal strand, stretching backwards, but looping round to arrive where we began. We shall, to some extent, be time travellers, coming and going on our biblical route, tracing and retracing the path of salvation as we approach the birth of Christ via the events of his resurrection, death and life.

In the life of faith we hold all the events of Christ's life together, knowing them all at once, it seems, and yet we invariably journey only in the linear direction that begins with Old Testament prophecy and leads to his birth, childhood, ministry, death, resurrection and ascension. After these events, the Church is created, which carries us to the present day through the ongoing work of the Holy Spirit. This is the timeline with which we have been brought up in the faith and with which we are probably so familiar. It drives our liturgical year and enables us to travel through the seasons of Christmas, Lent, Easter and Pentecost in 'chronological' order. It is what I, and perhaps you, have done all our lives, and it is good to do. Yet, this Advent and Christmas, I invite you to turn around and travel in the opposite direction, going against the flow, for then the view will be different.

On the other track, as it were, we shall also visit some real and significant places. As well as travelling in time, I want to travel in space to the locations in which scripture and tradition have placed the events of Jesus' life, death and resurrection. Many of these places can be visited today, and the Holy Lands of Israel, Palestine and Jordan have been pilgrimage destinations for centuries since the first pilgrim, Egeria, travelled to the lands of Christ around AD381–384.

Visiting pilgrimage sites today can be a profound experience or it can summon feelings of resentment or annoyance, as commercialisation, fiction, wishful thinking, exploitation and devotional extravagance are often in evidence. Some sites are clearly genuine, others utterly spurious. Some conjure up a wonderful sense of sacred space without laying much claim to authenticity, while others have their authenticity spoiled by the attitudes and practices on display within them. We shall 'visit' some of these sites, in an attempt to decipher their old stones, and you can make up your own mind. Perhaps you have visited them in person or may yet be inspired to do so. I have been fortunate over the years to join with and lead pilgrimages to Israel, Palestine, Egypt, Turkey and Jordan, with the wise assistance of McCabe Travel, who are one of several companies that understand the modern dynamics of the Middle East well enough to ensure that safe, pleasant and wonderfully uplifting trips can be had at very reasonable cost. On pilgrimages with both parishioners and clergy, I have found that such trips foster fellowship, facilitate great learning and, inevitably, bring everyone face to face with the challenging realities of life and politics in the modern Middle East. If one has visited these places, and met, spoken to and eaten with the people who are sometimes known as the 'living stones' of the Holy Land, the news bulletins come across very differently.

As mentioned above, this winter journey, through December and into the new year, is a virtual pilgrimage whose itinerary heads backwards in time. Real pilgrimages do that, too: the events of the Gospels have a chronology and they have locations, but it is not always practical to visit sites in the order found in the biblical accounts. A real pilgrimage jumps about all over the place, visiting sites for their geographical proximity, which means that a pilgrim has to juggle their prior knowledge and their new experiences to be sorted and ordered and reflected upon later. Yet, whose life is not a juggling feat? Whose life is so well ordered that everything falls into place just as we would like? Our lives, pilgrimages as they ultimately are, take many turns, and we are constantly revisiting experiences and places from the past and therefore, of course, of the future.

In the end, it is our burden and our joy, guided by God's Holy Spirit, to make sense of our comings and goings and to stay faithful to Christ as we navigate the zigzag path that stretches both forwards to the end and backwards to the beginning.

1 December

The beginning of the end and the 'four last things'

'When you see Jerusalem surrounded by armies, then know that its desolation has come near. Then those in Judea must flee to the mountains, and those inside the city must leave it, and those out in the country must not enter it; for these are days of vengeance, as a fulfilment of all that is written. Woe to those who are pregnant and to those who are nursing infants in those days! For there will be great distress on the earth and wrath against this people; they will fall by the edge of the sword and be taken away as captives among all nations; and Jerusalem will be trampled on by the Gentiles, until the times of the Gentiles are fulfilled. There will be signs in the sun, the moon, and the stars, and on the earth distress among nations confused by the roaring of the sea and the waves. People will faint from fear and foreboding of what is coming upon the world, for the powers of the heavens will be shaken. Then they will see "the Son of Man coming in a cloud" with power and great glory. Now when these things begin to take place, stand up and raise your heads, because your redemption is drawing near.'

LUKE 21:20–28

In Advent we mark the beginning of the church year (most lectionaries commence today), and we do so by focusing on the end of time. Endings and beginnings combine as we enter

Advent, and it can be a little disorientating. While everyone else is looking forward to Christmas (an event in the past), the church is trying to get back to the future, to some point at which we suppose prophecies like these words of Jesus will come true or, in some other sense, be fulfilled. The fact that Jesus' prophecy about Jerusalem did come true in AD70 adds confusion to our comings and goings, up and down and through the Bible. The future that Jesus is referring to here is, in fact, way back in the past.

Jesus was speaking some time around AD30; his words were recorded and were written down by Luke some time around AD80–100. This means, of course, that Jerusalem had already been 'trampled on by Gentiles' when Luke committed these sayings to paper. The first Jewish–Roman war raged between AD66 and 73, having begun with protests about Roman taxation in Judea, which led to the Romans massacring 6000 Jews in Jerusalem. Full-scale rebellion ensued and the Jews initially succeeded against strong opposition. In AD70, however, after a terrible seven-month siege, the walls of Jerusalem were breached by the Romans. Led by Titus (Roman Emperor from 79 to 81), they burned and ransacked the city, including the temple (only recently completed, in AD64), with the exception of three towers and part of the Western Wall, still referred to by some as the Wailing Wall.

The desolation of Jerusalem in AD70 resonates with the passage from Luke's Gospel with which we begin our journey into the past. It looks like prophecy and would have sounded like a premonition to Jesus' hearers. We might say that Jesus could predict the future, and we might say that he was a shrewd judge of what he saw around him: he lived among zealots and Romans, enemies who laid different claims to the holy city and its surrounding territories. His own crucifixion came as a direct result of one faction (the Jewish religious authorities) playing on the fears of another (the Romans). The seeds of rebellion were already planted in the 30s, and the writing of rebellion was already on the wall. So Jesus' warning about what would happen to Jerusalem made a lot of sense to his hearers, and even more sense to Luke, after it had happened. There can be little doubt that, as the walls came tumbling down and the starving inhabitants were put to the sword, it did feel like the end of the world to those who witnessed it, both in Jerusalem in AD70 and in Masada three years later, when the Jewish revolt was finally crushed. Jesus saw it all coming.

We are not only beginning with the end, but we are also in the most significant place. Jerusalem is the 'holy city', revered by three major religions, all of which share a common ancestry in Abraham, who was effectively the founder of Jerusalem. In the 19th century BC the Egyptians had called it Urusalimum. A semitic (Hebrew) variation on this name, Urusalim, can be traced to the Egyptian city of Tel al Armana in the 14th century BC. The Assyrian King Sennacherib called it Ursalimmu in the seventh century BC and, although he tried to invade and capture it, he never succeeded (see 2 Kings 19:15–34). These original names were made up of the words *uru*, meaning 'city', and *Salim*, a name for a god. Thus, Jerusalem has always been known as a city of a god, but not the God of the Hebrews, the God of Abraham and Isaac and Jesus Christ: Salim was an Amorite god, whose name lives on in the Jerusalem of today.

Abraham (Abram) is the person with whom Jerusalem is first associated in Genesis, when Melchizedek, the archetypal first high priest of the one and only God, greets him there, offering him bread and wine in a gesture of friendship and fellowship (Genesis 14:17–20). Abraham's nephew, Lot, has been captured in a battle near the Dead Sea, so his uncle attacks King Chedorlaomer's invaders to restore order. Melchizedek thanks him, recognising that he is also a worshipper of the singular creator God. Abraham responds with a tithe (a tenth of everything, v. 19), cementing his key role as the father of monotheistic faith. The story is quoted in Hebrews 7:1–10, which relates Jesus to a priestly succession that goes right back to Abraham's encounter with Melchizedek on a spot that is pivotal in world history.

In Jewish tradition, Jerusalem is the place where the world was created and where Adam was made from the soil of the earth. The golden Dome of the Rock, which sits atop the Temple Mount in Jerusalem to this day, is revered as the very spot where the Holy of Holies was situated, the room in the temple where the ark of the covenant was kept. Both Muslims and Jews believe that this is also the site, then called Mount Moriah, where Abraham was told to sacrifice Isaac (in Islamic tradition the story relates to Isaac's half-brother, Ishmael). For Christians, Jerusalem is the place where Jesus taught, and it is the holy city of his crucifixion and resurrection.

So it is right that we begin our journey at the end times, in Jerusalem, for in Jerusalem all things begin and end, are destroyed and renewed.

In vain the surge's angry shock,
in vain the drifting sands;
unharmed upon the eternal Rock
the eternal City stands.
SAMUEL JOHNSON (1822–82)

2 December

Death comes to us all

What I am saying, brothers and sisters, is this: flesh and blood cannot inherit the kingdom of God, nor does the perishable inherit the imperishable. Listen, I will tell you a mystery! We will not all die, but we will all be changed, in a moment, in the twinkling of an eye, at the last trumpet. For the trumpet will sound, and the dead will be raised imperishable, and we will be changed. For this perishable body must put on imperishability, and this mortal body must put on immortality. When this perishable body puts on imperishability, and this mortal body puts on immortality, then the saying that is written will be fulfilled: 'Death has been swallowed up in victory.' 'Where, O death, is your victory? Where, O death, is your sting?'

1 CORINTHIANS 15:50–55

There is a tradition in Advent of reflection on the 'four last things'—death, judgement, hell and heaven. Many people have mixed feelings about these, two of which are ostensibly places and two of which are moments in time. Yet even mention of them causes us to reflect upon what 'time' and 'place' really are.

Nothing focuses the mind more than death, which, it seems both logical and traditional to suppose, precedes judgement, hell and heaven, whatever they might be. And whatever one thinks or believes about these last three, there is no one who doesn't believe in death. Around 150,000 people die every day worldwide, yet death is life's great mystery. We do not fully understand what happens, how it happens or why it happens. 'In the midst of life we are in death'; we cannot avoid it, neither on our TV screens nor in our own families. Death comes to us all, and we are changed by it. It is often said that to live is to change, but it is also true, as Paul tells us, that to die is to be changed (v. 52). This change is something that happens to us, not something we do ourselves.

If birth is the coming of life, then death is its going. In that we ask questions about when life begins, we take for granted that each of our lives has a beginning. We assume that there was some point in time before which we did not exist in any form. Many people now take the view that we return to that state of non-existence when we die. Our lives seem to occupy the temporal space between two moments— the moment of coming into being and the moment of going into not-being. How we fill that time is our choice and our chance, and how long it will last is an unknown quantity. As the psalmist wrote, 'Lord, let me know my end, and what is the measure of my days; let me know how fleeting my life is. You have made my days a few handbreadths, and my lifetime is as nothing in your sight' (Psalm 39:4–5). Nowadays some people do know how much longer they have to live: terminal illness diagnosis and palliative care predictions are sometimes accurate, and the ability to prepare for the immediacy of one's passing—physically, mentally, emotionally and spiritually—is a gift, or curse, of science.

No scientist or linguist can tell us, though, what it is that we are 'passing' to. This word we use to gloss over death reflects our unease with—or denial of—the final reality of someone's disappearance from the presence of those with whom they have occupied physical space and emotional time. Death is an ending, for sure, for those left behind, at the very least. In death our earthly lives are over, and no euphemism will conceal that reality.

On the other hand, death does not make sense, philosophically. Augustine of Hippo (354–430) realised that there is a problem with talking about the past as 'that which has happened' and the future as 'that which will happen'. It leaves no space for the present, or, rather, it begs a question about exactly how long 'now' lasts. More recently, the Czech immunologist and poet Miroslav Holub (1923–98) suggested that the present moment lasts about three seconds before it becomes an event in the past. Everything that happens happens in the now; it does not and cannot actually happen in the past or the future. Every event that ever was or will be happens in a 'now' at the time. Time seems to flow, therefore, from one 'now' to the next, approaching future 'nows' and consigning the present to the past as it flows.

This process may get us through life in a vaguely satisfactory manner, but we know that time can be divided into segments far briefer than three seconds. Furthermore, how long does it take to die? We cannot answer that question unless we can define 'life', and that, the medics will tell you, is not so easy. What they do tell us is that death should be thought of more as a process than as an event. Nevertheless, they will also tell us that clinical death occurs when the heart stops pumping blood and breathing ceases. Consciousness is lost within several seconds, while measurable brain activity continues for only 20–40 seconds. The tissues begin to be starved of oxygen and, within a few minutes, can be irreversibly damaged by a process known as ischemia.

None of these symptoms of death is momentary, and, when observing them, it is far easier to say, for example, that brain activity has ceased (and therefore death has occurred) than that brain activity is in the process of ceasing (so someone is not yet dead but soon will be).

Mind-boggling as this is, we are still wedded spiritually and culturally to the idea that there is a moment of death. We cannot say for certain what it is to die, so whatever happens 'next' is even more problematic. However, those who say that death is the end have even less to inform their view than the resurrection hope in which Christians believe. In life and in death we are for ever changing; we are born, we grow, we flourish, but then we also ail, weaken and die. Such is the nature of things. Yet it is God who, as Creator, gives us life and gives us hope in eternal life as death disconnects us from this earthly realm. It is God who gives us Jesus Christ, in whose victory death itself is swallowed up, reconnecting us to both the earthly and the eternal.

When we die we are changed, and we should not despair. We are in the hands of God, and we should remember that death has been swallowed up in the victory of Christ. We do not know what eternity and resurrection are like, but we do know that they are not nothing. Our Christian hope is that death is not the end, and there is something to live and die and hope for.

I fear no foe, with Thee at hand to bless;
Ills have no weight, and tears no bitterness.
Where is death's sting? Where, grave, thy victory?
I triumph still, if Thou abide with me.
HENRY FRANCIS LYTE (1793–1847)

3 December

Christ comes in judgement

'When the Son of Man comes in his glory, and all the angels with him, then he will sit on the throne of his glory. All the nations will be gathered before him, and he will separate people one from another as a shepherd separates the sheep from the goats, and he will put the sheep at his right hand and the goats at the left. Then the king will say to those at his right hand, "Come, you that are blessed by my Father, inherit the kingdom prepared for you from the foundation of the world; for I was hungry and you gave me food, I was thirsty and you gave me something to drink, I was a stranger and you welcomed me, I was naked and you gave me clothing, I was sick and you took care of me, I was in prison and you visited me." Then the righteous will answer him, "Lord, when was it that we saw you hungry and gave you food, or thirsty and gave you something to drink? And when was it that we saw you a stranger and welcomed you, or naked and gave you clothing? And when was it that we saw you sick or in prison and visited you?" And the king will answer them, "Truly I tell you, just as you did it to one of the least of these who are members of my family, you did it to me." Then he will say to those at his left hand, "You that are accursed, depart from me into the eternal fire prepared for the devil and his angels; for I was hungry and you gave me no food, I was thirsty and you gave me nothing to drink, I was a stranger and you did not welcome me, naked and you did not give

me clothing, sick and in prison and you did not visit me."...
"Truly I tell you, just as you did not do it to one of the least of
these, you did not do it to me." And these will go away into
eternal punishment, but the righteous into eternal life.'
MATTHEW 25:31–43, 45–46

When we have died (whatever that actually involves), what
happens next? Are we 'going' to heaven or hell? Before we
can consider what those two 'places' or destinations on our
journey might be, we must turn our attention to the second
of the 'four last things'—judgement. This parable of the
sheep and the goats is a wonderfully simple but powerful
summary of what Christians have believed for centuries
about what happens when we die. Some things in the parable
are clear: there are two destinations or states to end up in,
eternal life or eternal punishment. Both entail some kind
of continuation, which may be anticipated with something
between complacency and terror. It is clear that the scenario
Jesus paints is familiar to his original hearers. The parable is
not about what heaven or hell is *like*: they know that already.
Jesus' point is to indicate on what grounds the determination
of destination is achieved.

It is important to understand that, in first-century
Palestine, sheep and goats were regarded as essentially the
same animal; they were not distinguished from each other,
as they are in our culture. Just as wheat and tares (a kind of
weed) would be allowed to grow together (Matthew 13:24–
30), to be separated at harvest time, sheep and goats would
graze together. Ultimately God makes distinctions that we
do not; when those distinctions are made, and because we
cannot tell the difference between sheep and goats, there will
be an element of surprise.

Even more important in this parable is the rationale behind the day of judgement. Notwithstanding what Paul and James wrote to their friends and followers in Greece and Rome about salvation through faith rather than works, here it is very clear: where you go when you die depends on how you have lived, and the 'good guys' are those who have shown compassion and care for the weak and vulnerable. The message is simple: if you cared for them, you will be saved; if you did not, woe betide you.

Consequently, in the medieval Western Church, the emphasis at funerals moved away from the hope of eternal life to an emphasis on judgement, with hell and purgatory very much in evidence. Funerals became public events at which the church attempted to discipline the people, and artists depicted the torments of the damned and the rewards of the faithful. In 1533, Pope Clement VII asked Michelangelo to paint *The Last Judgement* on the wall behind the altar in the Sistine Chapel, commissioning one of the most vivid depictions of Jesus' parable. Similarly, 'mystery plays' portrayed the souls of the damned being dragged into hell, and Dante emphasised the idea in his *Inferno*. Musically, Requiem masses, especially those by Berlioz and Verdi, rendered this terrifying moment in a blaze of multiphonic awe. In poetry we only have to turn to 'The Dream of Gerontius' by Cardinal Newman (set so marvellously to music by Sir Edward Elgar) to enter into the experience of judgement as filtered by the medieval church. Newman's text describes how the old man Gerontius makes confession and passes from life to death, going via purgatory to heaven.

Protestants do not believe in purgatory. The 22nd of the 39 Articles of Religion describe it as 'a fond thing vainly invented' and, indeed, many Roman Catholics have abandoned it too. Karl Rahner, probably the greatest Catholic theologian of the 20th century, was not very interested in the particular salvation of a particular soul, where it happened and when and how; rather, he focused on the idea that after death the soul is united with the cosmos, through which, while awaiting the final day of resurrection, the soul becomes aware of the effects of sin on the world. This, Rahner reckoned, would be purgatory enough—not so much punishment as awareness. More significant still is the opinion of Pope Benedict XVI (Josef Ratzinger). He did not like the classical, pay-and-display-your-sins idea of a middle stage between death and salvation. Rather, he believed that Jesus himself is the refining fire who transforms us in the power of resurrection. Significantly, this is a doctrine of death and judgement that relates to Jesus Christ rather than to human prayer and intervention, indulgences and all the medieval paraphernalia of devotion that sought to scare people out of hell by 'scaring the hell' out of them.

Even more important, in this movement away from medieval understandings about judgement, is our renewed ability to return to resurrection hope. Jesus told the parable of the sheep and goats in order to show that God makes distinctions that we do not, and to promote compassion and love for neighbours. Not long after this parable, we read that he went on to suffer and die, before rising again. Christianity bases its fundamental hope on resurrection, not on the immortality of the soul. Christ leads us in that way by his own victory over death. Whatever 'judgement' is or however it happens, our calling as Christians is to love our neighbours and trust in God's merciful redemption, which leads to resurrection life.

When I needed a neighbour, were you there, were you there?...
I was hungry and thirsty, were you there, were you there?...
I was cold, I was naked, were you there, were you there?...
When I needed a shelter, were you there, were you there?...

SIDNEY CARTER (1915–2004)

4 December

Going to hell

'There was a rich man who was dressed in purple and fine linen and who feasted sumptuously every day. And at his gate lay a poor man named Lazarus, covered with sores, who longed to satisfy his hunger with what fell from the rich man's table; even the dogs would come and lick his sores. The poor man died and was carried away by the angels to be with Abraham. The rich man also died and was buried. In Hades, where he was being tormented, he looked up and saw Abraham far away with Lazarus by his side. He called out, "Father Abraham, have mercy on me, and send Lazarus to dip the tip of his finger in water and cool my tongue; for I am in agony in these flames." But Abraham said, "Child, remember that during your lifetime you received your good things, and Lazarus in like manner evil things; but now he is comforted here, and you are in agony. Besides all this, between you and us a great chasm has been fixed, so that those who might want to pass from here to you cannot do so, and no one can cross from there to us."'

LUKE 16:19–26

It is possible to go to Hell. Known in Jesus' day as Gehenna, it is a valley on the south side of Jerusalem, where children were once sacrificed to the god Molech (2 Kings 23:10). It became a rubbish tip and was perpetually on fire, thereby presenting an image to which people could relate. Consequently the

23

valley was considered accursed, and 'Gehenna' became a synonym for hell. It can be seen today from the vantage point of Caiaphas' House (also known as St Peter in Galicantu), which marks the place where Peter denied knowing Jesus three times (Mark 14:66–72).

If Gehenna was a real place where grotesque violence was known to have happened, we can add to the mix the Jewish concept of Sheol, the place of the dead. According to Job 11:8, this was a very deep place, as far away from heaven as it could be. It seems to have had various compartments or regions, and there was a sense of life continuing there in some way. Jacob expected to mourn there (Genesis 37:35); David gave instructions not to let his army commander, Joab, go there in peace (1 Kings 2:6); soldiers took their weapons to Sheol with them (Ezekiel 32:27), yet the dead existed there without knowledge or feeling, in silence and oblivion. Significantly, it was not believed to be completely separated from God; indeed, God could reach into it (Amos 9:2).

As well as Gehenna and Sheol, we need to introduce the mythological idea of Hades into our dark and deadly equation. The Greek god Hades, son of Cronus and Rhea, received the underworld for his realm when his brother gods, Zeus and Poseidon, received dominion of the sky and sea respectively. This underworld realm soon became known simply as Hades. It was not considered a place of torment; rather, it was a sad dreamworld, without daylight or hope, where the dead would fade away. Hades was surrounded by five rivers: the Acheron (river of woe), the Cocytus (river of lamentation), the Phlegethon (river of fire), the Styx (river of unbreakable oaths), and the Lethe (river of forgetfulness). Thus, ancient Greek thought (in which the apostle Paul would have been well schooled) had developed an understanding of a gloomy underworld populated by mournful souls consigned to oblivion.

As we arrive at the medieval idea of hell, it is clear that elements of Sheol, Hades and Gehenna have combined to influence our culture and our interpretation of what it might mean to be judged and 'go to hell'. The medieval picture, which so many people today find difficult to engage with, was planted in Western culture by the Italian poet Dante Alighieri (c.1265–1321), whose *Divine Comedy* is undoubtedly one of the greatest and most influential poems ever written. Divided into three parts, *'Inferno'*, *'Purgatorio'* and *'Paradiso'*, it lays out an allegorical journey from death to redemption, cementing in popular imagination the idea that if a person recognised their sin, they could pass through a purging place (purgatory) and be made fit for heaven subsequently.

The schema depends on concepts of both time and place that are far from earthly. 'Inferno' (literally 'fire'), or Hell, is divided into nine layers or circles, each reserved for the perpetrators of certain kinds of sins—Limbo, Lust, Gluttony, Greed, Anger, Heresy, Violence, Fraud and Treachery. Limbo, famously and controversially, contained the unbaptised and virtuous pagans, who, though not sinful, had not accepted Christ. They were not tormented as such; the torments of Hell escalated through the other circles. Dante's vision was extensive and rich, and he populated his Hell with real and imagined characters. At the epicentre of Hell was a giant, terrifying beast with three faces, one red, one black and one a pale yellow—none other than Satan himself, condemned for his personal treachery against God, the ultimate sin.

Another brief reference to hell is to be found in 2 Peter 2:4: 'For if God did not spare the angels when they sinned, but cast them into hell and committed them to chains of deepest darkness to be kept until the judgement...'. Here the Greek word for hell is *tartaros* (which found its way into the Latin Requiem texts set to music by many composers).

When we think about hell, then, we are considering a conglomeration of traditions. Only some of these traditions originate in the Bible, and some of them are works of fiction. Nevertheless, in Jesus' parable of the rich man and Lazarus, this stereotypical 'up or down', 'burn or bask' presentation of the afterlife is clear to behold. The name Lazarus is a variant of Eleazar, which means 'God has helped'. This Lazarus is not to be confused with Lazarus of Bethany, the brother of Mary and Martha, whom Jesus raised from the dead in John 11. This Lazarus was a friend of Jesus, and the other didn't really exist: he is merely a character in a parable.

In comparing the two Lazaruses in the New Testament, we encounter a difficult puzzle. The Lazarus in the parable is enjoying what might be considered to be the eternal life of his soul. He has died and gone to heaven. His nemesis, the rich man, has died and gone to the other place. This situation is clear-cut, black and white, but it flies in the face of what happened to the other Lazarus, whom Jesus raised from the dead. We are not told that Lazarus of Bethany died and went to heaven; rather, he was raised from the dead—a physical resurrection. In that story, and in his own death and resurrection, Jesus shows us a foretaste not of heaven but of resurrection life.

Can we reconcile the two? Do we have the eternal life of the soul, whereby the body rots and the soul lives on in paradise or hell, or do we look to resurrection—the raising of our bodies on the last day, to be united with Christ and to dwell with saints and angels? In the communion of saints, of which we are *already* a part, we experience resurrection life rather than the simple 'eternal life' of a disembodied soul.

Tomorrow we shall ascend to heaven to see if we can find out.

Brief life is here our portion, brief sorrow, short lived care;
The life that knows no ending, the tearless life, is there.
O happy retribution! Short toil, eternal rest;
For mortals and for sinners, a mansion with the blest.

BERNARD OF MORLAIX, 1146

5 December

Going to heaven

Then I saw a new heaven and a new earth; for the first heaven and the first earth had passed away, and the sea was no more. And I saw the holy city, the new Jerusalem, coming down out of heaven from God, prepared as a bride adorned for her husband. And I heard a loud voice from the throne saying,

'See, the home of God is among mortals. He will dwell with them; they will be his peoples, and God himself will be with them; he will wipe every tear from their eyes. Death will be no more; mourning and crying and pain will be no more, for the first things have passed away.'

And the one who was seated on the throne said, 'See, I am making all things new.' Also he said, 'Write this, for these words are trustworthy and true.' Then he said to me, 'It is done! I am the Alpha and the Omega, the beginning and the end. To the thirsty I will give water as a gift from the spring of the water of life. Those who conquer will inherit these things, and I will be their God and they will be my children. But as for the cowardly, the faithless, the polluted, the murderers, the fornicators, the sorcerers, the idolaters, and all liars, their place will be in the lake that burns with fire and sulphur, which is the second death.'

REVELATION 21:1–8

Yesterday we were in hell; today we go to heaven. Here we are, at the beginning of our Advent journey, arriving at our ultimate destination. We stand in the future: the world has ended, tribulation is over and whatever ecological or cosmological catastrophe it was that ended life on earth has passed. Now the old city of God is transformed and a 'new' Jerusalem is inaugurated as an embodiment of human hope for an eternal dwelling place in the presence of God. It is a truly glorious place, with jasper walls, pearly gates and streets of gold. The tree of life grows there, and through the city flows the river of life, yet it lacks sun, moon, day and night and there is no temple. Nevertheless, as in the parable of Lazarus and the rich man, there is also a darker overtone—a reference to another place, another death, an eternal, burning lake for the dishonest and the despicable.

We may be able to picture these fantastical horrors and wonders, but there is a deeper meaning too. In the Old Testament, the temple represented the aspirations of the nation and the presence of God. Many of the prophets saw Jerusalem decline as the people sinned, but Isaiah and Ezekiel had visions of reconstruction. John's visionary revelation is the culmination of a tradition of divinely assisted rise and fall and rebirth that gained ground in the inter-testamental period. Jesus himself refers to this tradition when predicting the fall of Jerusalem: 'Do you see these great buildings? Not one stone will be left here upon another; all will be thrown down... Then they will see "the Son of Man coming in clouds" with great power and glory' (Mark 13:2, 26).

In Greek there are two words that we translate as 'new'. When a city is rebuilt, it is new, but John sees a 'new' Jerusalem that is clean and pure, cleansed and different, heralding a new order. This is more than surface novelty but something deep down, spiritually rather than simply physically 'new'. The same sense is found in the 'New'

Testament or covenant, as well as the new creation. In fact, it is Christ, the Son of God and redeemer of the world, who is the new Jerusalem, in whom all things are made new, and the history of Jerusalem is, in a sense, the story of that renewal. The new Jerusalem is the city of God, and the city of God is heaven, the place of pleasure and rest and union to which we all aspire, especially in contrast to the 'other' place of pain and despair.

Just as the heritage of hell contains elements of Jewish, Greek and medieval Christian tradition, so too does the heritage of heaven. While the ancient Greeks had Hades to fear, they had Elysium to look forward to. Medieval Europe made heaven a great reward, in contrast to hell, which was construed as constant punishment for sinful deeds. These deeds may have been wicked but they were finite and bounded by earthly time; yet temporal sin had eternal consequences. The medieval church was quite specific about the nature and the implications of all sorts of different sinful deeds: as we saw yesterday, Dante suggested special levels of hell for different kinds of sinners.

Whatever we say about heaven or hell, as places or eternal time zones (for traditions suggest they are both), we have to get to grips with the ideas of body and soul that Greco-Roman-Judeo-Christian cultures have inherited, adopted and developed over the centuries. These philosophies have continued to develop well beyond the Enlightenment movement of the 18th century and the postmodernism of the late 20th century.

The idea of the disembodied soul is a carry-over from Greek mythology and philosophy. Western culture has been influenced by it greatly, both because of and in spite of what the church has taught and believed, and even misunderstood, for centuries. It was the ancient Greek philosopher Plato who encouraged his readers to think in terms of a separation between the mind and body, along with an approach that distinguishes between reality and idealism. That is to say, he believed that while we have real things, such as tables, chairs, knives and forks, all of them are imperfect realisations of the 'ideal' chair, table, knife or fork that exist in a non-physical realm. Connected to this is the idea that our lives are some kind of imperfect realisation of who we really are, should be or will be.

Plato's protégé Aristotle became tutor to Alexander the Great, whose military and intellectual influence was vast. The apostle Paul was also influenced by ancient Greek thought, as adopted, understood and adapted by the intellectual rabbinic tradition in which he, as a committed, learned Jew, was brought up before he dramatically met Christ on the road to Damascus. Consequently, the idea of soul/body dualism has travelled through Western thought alongside the Easter stories. This inherited dualism manifests itself in parables as ancient as 'the rich man and Lazarus', to make a point about how we live our lives, given that there is a realm beyond this one, in which consequences of actions, justice and mercy are real.

Simultaneously, in Christ we are promised a hope of bodily resurrection as experienced briefly by the other Lazarus, Jesus' friend. I suspect that this is a 'both–and', not an 'either–or' situation. Jesus brought resurrection life to the real Lazarus, but used his fictional Lazarus to speak into a culture that believed in a disembodied afterlife. Resurrection life is better than afterlife. God, our creator and redeemer and sustainer, does not have to understand things the way we do; nor does he answer to the demands of our enquiry or the constraints of the human mind. Paul, the classically educated Jewish scholar and Christian convert, reminds us that ultimately we are dealing in mystery—things that words cannot adequately describe—and this is never more true than when we are contemplating the great mystery of eternal, bodily resurrection life:

> *Listen, I will tell you a mystery! We will not all fall asleep, but we will all be changed, in a moment, in the twinkling of an eye, at the last trumpet. For the trumpet will sound, and the dead will be raised imperishable, and we will be changed.*
>
> 1 CORINTHIANS 15:51–52

> *My flesh in hope shall rest,*
> *And for a season slumber:*
> *Till trump from east to west*
> *Shall wake the dead in number*
>
> GEORGE RATCLIFFE WOODWARD (1848–1934)

6 December

Paul goes to Damascus

Now as [Saul] was going along and approaching Damascus, suddenly a light from heaven flashed around him. He fell to the ground and heard a voice saying to him, 'Saul, Saul, why do you persecute me?' He asked, 'Who are you, Lord?' The reply came, 'I am Jesus, whom you are persecuting. But get up and enter the city, and you will be told what you are to do.' The men who were travelling with him stood speechless because they heard the voice but saw no one. Saul got up from the ground, and though his eyes were open, he could see nothing; so they led him by the hand and brought him into Damascus. For three days he was without sight, and neither ate nor drank.

ACTS 9:3–9

We begin our journey back through the Bible with the conversion of Saul to Paul—one of the key moments in world history. Although we might not want to agree completely with those who say he 'founded' or even 'invented' Christianity, there can be no doubt that Paul's influence was massive and that the church as we know it evolved in a very Pauline way. To put it differently, God used this zealous, overbearing, possibly rather unpleasant religious fanatic to propel the message and meaning of Christ into the geography of the first century and the history of the world. Without Paul, Christianity would not have 'taken off' as it did, and it might not have survived for long. It certainly would not be what it is today.

Yet all counterfactuals are false, as the philosophers put it. That is to say, we can never know what might have happened had something *not* been the case, and so we cannot prove that things would have been different under other circumstances. The 'if onlys' of history cannot be verified, and we cannot live by them or believe in something that never happened. Instead, we stick to what we do know, and live by that.

We know, for he tells us himself (in Galatians 1:11–16), that Saul was a zealous Jew who had a very strange, life-changing experience on his way to Damascus. We know what he did as a result, and we know that it made him somewhat distrusted at first (Acts 9:26). In his approach to mission, he clashed with Simon Peter (Galatians 2:11–14) and disagreed with Barnabas to the extent that they went their separate ways (Acts 15:36–39). On the Damascus road, Paul was temporarily blinded and his focus changed, but his character, determination and commitment to the cause were realigned rather than removed by God. In the world of mission and evangelism that Paul was to carve out, his strong, uncompromising character was just what was needed.

For this reason, there are some Christians who find Paul hard to take. His attitude towards women and his perceived illiberality offend those who prefer to focus on the love and mercy of God. Some argue that, because he was so rooted in the Greek and Jewish culture of his day, some of his instructions to the various communities to which he wrote were specific and timebound, and are therefore irrelevant today.

For sure, the influence of Paul on the Christian faith is

powerful and profound. His journeys and teachings, written down by Luke in the Acts of the Apostles and recorded in his own correspondence with fledgling church communities, are vital to our understanding of who Jesus is and what God has done for us in him. Paul's letters are the oldest Christian documents: they predate the Gospel writers' work. For example, the first published account of what Jesus did with bread and wine is actually to be found in one of Paul's letters, in which he writes, 'For I received from the Lord what I also handed on to you, that the Lord Jesus on the night when he was betrayed took a loaf of bread, and when he had given thanks, he broke it and said, "This is my body that is for you. Do this in remembrance of me"' (1 Corinthians 11:23–24). Some of what we know about Jesus, including the first interpretations of his being and teaching, come to us first through Paul. If the New Testament were set out in the order in which the texts were actually written, it would seem quite disorientating to us now.

So it is fitting that, as we make a journey towards the beginning of time, we encounter Paul before we meet Jesus on our own roads of faith. This is exactly what so many of the early Christians did. They met Paul and then heard about Jesus. The disciples who lived alongside Jesus focused on Jerusalem and Jewish converts, while Paul travelled and preached to Gentiles, non-Jews who had a very different perspective on life, the world and the universe.

It is also fitting that Paul was converted on a journey, for he was to become a journeyman for God. Widely travelled already, he was on his way to Damascus, 135 miles from Jerusalem. It is one of the oldest inhabited cities in the world, dating back to around 6300BC. In the time of Paul and of Jesus, it was one of ten cities annexed by the Romans and known as the Decapolis. In AD37 it was given by the Romans to the Nabateans (who are most famously associated with the city of Petra), but in AD106 the Romans defeated the Nabateans and reclaimed Damascus. It has been, at various times, a great city of Greek and Roman culture, of Christian teaching and faith, and of Islamic scholarship. The damage done to the city in the wake of civil war in Syria is a great sadness, but one from which it will surely recover. Ironically, it had become possible to visit Syria as a place of pilgrimage in the months before the civil war began in 2011, but we can only hope that peace may yet prevail and the road to Damascus will be opened again for all to see.

O glory most excelling
that smote across his path!
O light that pierced and blinded
the zealot in his wrath!
O voice that spake within him
the calm, reproving word!
O love that sought and held him
the bondman of his Lord!

JOHN ELLERTON (1826–93)

Stephen becomes a martyr in Jerusalem

When they heard these things, they became enraged and ground their teeth at Stephen. But filled with the Holy Spirit, he gazed into heaven and saw the glory of God and Jesus standing at the right hand of God. 'Look,' he said, 'I see the heavens opened and the Son of Man standing at the right hand of God!' But they covered their ears, and with a loud shout all rushed together against him. Then they dragged him out of the city and began to stone him; and the witnesses laid their coats at the feet of a young man named Saul. While they were stoning Stephen, he prayed, 'Lord Jesus, receive my spirit.' Then he knelt down and cried out in a loud voice, 'Lord, do not hold this sin against them.' When he had said this, he died. And Saul approved of their killing him. That day a severe persecution began against the church in Jerusalem.

ACTS 7:54—8:1A

Yesterday we met Paul, converted on the road to Damascus, having recently participated in the semi-official execution of a man who is now revered as the first Christian martyr. Like those in the Middle East (Asia Minor) who came to faith as a result of the preaching of Paul and his friends in the years after Jesus' death and resurrection, we are approaching the fantastical story of salvation through the doorway opened up by them. We do not yet know who this person Jesus is, or what really happened, but we are hearing of some very strange goings-on involving a zealous Jew named Saul. We have heard that he personally seeks out anyone converted to the new cult associated with Jesus Christ and supervises their trials and punishments.

In Jerusalem there was a man called Stephen, called by his brothers in Christ, along with Philip, Prochorus, Nicanor, Timon, Parmenas and Nicolaus, to be a deacon. Hands were laid upon them and the Holy Spirit invoked on their calling, which was to help the widows and serve at the tables as the poor were being fed. In modern terms, they were called by God and ordained to this task, after having been recognised by the community as the right people to meet the need, releasing others who would devote themselves to prayer and the ministry of the word (Acts 6:1–4). This idea of calling, ordination and devotion to prayer and ministry is still very much with us 2000 years later, especially in the calling of men and women in the church to be deacons. At the beginning of the Church of England ordination service, the bishop says, 'Deacons are ordained so that the people of God may be better equipped to make Christ known. Theirs is a life of visible self-giving. Christ is the pattern of their calling and their commission; as he washed the feet of his disciples, so they must wash the feet of others.' Later in the service, the bishop says, 'They are to proclaim the gospel in word and deed, as agents of God's purposes of love. They are to serve the community in which they are set, bringing to the Church the needs and hopes of all the people.'

As well as being honoured as the first Christian martyr, Stephen is recognised as one of the first seven Christian deacons, whose duties were not so different from those of deacons today. In the Church of England and the Roman

Catholic Church, as well as other denominations, priests are deacons too, and should not forget it. Deacons do not 'become' priests after a year or so. The calling is different, and some never do, yet all priests remain deacons (as do all bishops), and the call and duty to minister the word of God and care for the needy remains an inherent servanthood at the core of ordained ministry.

Stephen was called to serve and to preach. He was good at it—too good, it seems, for his wisdom made him enemies who sought to trap him and, in a very similar way to the manner in which Jesus was falsely accused, got the high priest to take an interest. Stephen's speech in Acts 7, which is more like a sermon, is a *tour de force* of biblical history, telling how God, through Abraham, Joseph and Moses and the prophets, sent word to his people to turn to him—but they would not, always resisting the work of the Holy Spirit. Finally, Stephen claims, his audience refused to listen to John proclaiming the coming of the Messiah and, ultimately, 'betrayed and murdered' Jesus (v. 52). At this point Stephen sees the risen Christ and quotes the prophet Daniel, which enrages his enemies even more, so much that they stone him.

The stoning of blasphemers or criminals was permitted under Jewish law, but the Romans would not have allowed it. Not long before, Jesus had had an encounter with a woman 'caught in adultery', and, although it seemed that the crowd intended to stone her, they did not carry out the threat, mostly because Jesus shamed them into going away (see John 8:1–11). On another occasion Jesus himself was nearly stoned by a lynch mob, but escaped (Luke 4:29, see 18 December; see also John 10:31–39). In Leviticus 24:13–16, the Law says that stoning is to be used in cases of blasphemy and should take place outside the city. The rabbinical tradition of Jewish law said that the criminal should be pushed face first from a precipice twice his height, on to rocks below. Then he would be turned over and, if he was not already dead, a second accuser would drop a large stone on his heart. If that did not do the job, then everyone else would join in. Legal or not, this is probably what they did to Stephen, and, in order to do so, they laid their cloaks at the feet of Saul, who was no doubt pleased to oversee a judicial killing for blasphemy. It certainly gave him added zeal for his persecution, which was instigated almost immediately.

There is no specific place to visit that claims to be the location of the stoning of Stephen, and the claim of St Stephen's Church in Jerusalem to hold his remains is probably spurious, based on the story of a priest named Lucian who, in 415, had a dream that revealed the location of Stephen's body. Nevertheless, the story of Stephen has both haunted and inspired the church ever since. Millions have been martyred over the centuries, and Stephen is their father in God. He is also father in God to all bishops, priests and deacons. He is an inspiration to all who would serve Jesus and who needs must die for their faith with the praise of Christ and forgiveness for others on their lips. Meanwhile, he is and will for ever be associated with that accursed Saul, beloved Paul, who shows us that even the vilest offender can yet be the greatest instrument of teaching, witness and evangelism.

Holy Spirit, gift of Jesus,
Shed thy light upon our eyes,
That we may behold with Stephen
That fair realm beyond the skies,
Where the Son of Man in glory
Waits for us at God's right hand,
King of saints and hope of martyrs,
Lord of all the pilgrim band.

CHRISTOPHER WORDSWORTH (1807–85)

8 December

The Spirit comes at Pentecost

When the day of Pentecost had come, they were all together in one place. And suddenly from heaven there came a sound like the rush of a violent wind, and it filled the entire house where they were sitting. Divided tongues, as of fire, appeared among them, and a tongue rested on each of them. All of them were filled with the Holy Spirit and began to speak in other languages, as the Spirit gave them ability. Now there were devout Jews from every nation under heaven living in Jerusalem. And at this sound the crowd gathered and was bewildered, because each one heard them speaking in the native language of each. Amazed and astonished, they asked, 'Are not all these who are speaking Galileans? And how is it that we hear, each of us, in our own native language?'
ACTS 2:1–8

Some traditions locate this great spiritual event in the very same room where Jesus had celebrated the last supper with his disciples before going out to the garden of Gethsemane to endure betrayal and arrest (Matthew 26:17–36). There is a nice roundness to the idea, although, as we can see above, the text does not specify that it was the same room. It is however a fair assumption, because we are told that when they gathered to elect Matthias to replace Judas as an apostle, 'When they had entered the city, they went to the room upstairs where they were staying' (Acts 1:13). So perhaps they were in that room when the day of Pentecost came, too.

Several significant events took place in the 50 days after the resurrection. 'Pentecost' is derived from the Greek word for the 50th day after Passover; in Jewish tradition, it is known as the Festival of Weeks, being seven weeks after Passover. The Christian church has developed a seven-week Eastertide liturgical season covering the period between Easter and Pentecost. What this means is that if the disciples were hiding out in the same upper room, it was only seven weeks after Jesus had sat among them and offered Passover bread and wine as his body and blood, telling them to continue the practice in remembrance of him.

In a sense, it would not have been only the disciples who were changed during this seven-week period, but the room itself. If we visit a historical monument—the Tower of London, for example—we can walk around, reflecting upon how much history its old walls have 'seen'. To consider the great historical events that have occurred in a particular place can be inspiring or, indeed, daunting. The Tower of London, one of the world's most famous prisons and now London's top tourist attraction, has been the location for dark events—the murder of the two princes and the beheadings of Anne Boleyn and Lady Jane Grey, to name but three.

Down the road is London's second most popular tourist attraction, St Paul's Cathedral, which has also seen a great wealth of history. It is a building with many personal memories for me: in the five-year period between 1998 and 2002, when I was a priest there, it was the setting for the Queen's Golden Jubilee services, the Queen Mother's 100th birthday service, national millennium services, and services marking the pain and tragedy of the September 11th attack in New York and the bombings in Bali soon after.

My wife and I were married there, and I helped to organise the memorial service for one of my colleagues' daughters, tragically knocked down in Fleet Street on 4 January 2000.

To others, St Paul's is the place that stood so resiliently against the Blitz in World War II; it hosted the funerals of Winston Churchill and Margaret Thatcher, and, perhaps most famously of all, the wedding of Lady Diana Spencer to Prince Charles. Further back in history, those not-so-ancient walls witnessed the funerals of Nelson and Wellington and the Diamond Jubilee service for Queen Victoria. Yet all of this pales against the thought that the very same upper room in Jerusalem may have witnessed the last supper and Pentecost. 'If only walls could speak,' we might say!

For many who visit the upper room (the Cenacle) in Jerusalem, it is as though its walls *can* speak. Although the room one visits today is not authentic, the site may be, and the Crusader-built room has a certain ambience, a simplicity that puts visitors in mind of the events attributed to it. So many sites in the Holy Land present the same difficulty and opportunity. People visit with a common purpose and feel a spirituality that has its origins, at the very least, somewhere close by. We do not know the exact location of the tongues of fire, but we are told they alighted somewhere in Jerusalem. If Pentecost is the birthday of the church, Jerusalem is the birthplace, and the Cenacle represents the very cradle of Christianity.

Meanwhile, we also know that Pentecost takes faith and religion away from specific places of worship and reverence. Pentecost was the beginning of an outward movement as the disciples drew inspiration (and remembered the injunction) to spread the good news of the saving death and resurrection of Jesus. Pentecost is about the Spirit dwelling everywhere, not just in one place or one city. The disciples, frightened Jews, had shut themselves away in a room above street level, hiding from the Roman and religious authorities. Whatever happened in that room, though, turned their inward-looking fear into outgoing, witnessing courage. It turned men and women who had seen their best friend crucified into martyrs—witnesses not only to that death but also to the resurrection events that followed, for which they themselves became willing to give up their own lives. Most of them did so.

Pentecost signifies the birth of the Church, because from it spreads out and advances the movement that the apostle Paul eventually embraced, which we know as Christianity. This faith remains the single greatest force for good in history and the most significant religion the planet has seen, and to some extent it all began in that secluded upper room in the heart of Jerusalem.

> *Thou giv'st the Holy Spirit's dower,*
> *Spirit of life and love and power,*
> *And does his sevenfold graces shower*
> *Upon us all.*
> CHRISTOPHER WORDSWORTH (1807–85)

9 December

Going to the Father on the Mount of Olives

So when they had come together, they asked him, 'Lord, is this the time when you will restore the kingdom to Israel?' He replied, 'It is not for you to know the times or periods that the Father has set by his own authority. But you will receive power when the Holy Spirit has come upon you; and you will be my witnesses in Jerusalem, in all Judea and Samaria, and to the ends of the earth.' When he had said this, as they were watching, he was lifted up, and a cloud took him out of their sight. While he was going and they were gazing up towards heaven, suddenly two men in white robes stood by them. They said, 'Men of Galilee, why do you stand looking up towards heaven? This Jesus, who has been taken up from you into heaven, will come in the same way as you saw him go into heaven.' Then they returned to Jerusalem from the mount called Olivet, which is near Jerusalem, a sabbath day's journey away.

ACTS 1:6–12

We begin our reverse journey into the life of Jesus at the point of farewell. Gathered on the Mount of Olives once again, in what is the closest thing to a funeral for Jesus that we might imagine, Jesus is taken from the disciples' sight and they are left to await the sending of the Holy Spirit. One might wonder if they shed tears in this place where Jesus had done so, only a few weeks earlier (Luke 19:41). Like mourners at a funeral, they remain rooted to the spot, needing to begin the process of moving on into a new reality, fuelled by hope and memory. It is an emotional moment in a significant place.

The Mount of Olives, sometimes called Olivet, is the hill on the east side of Jerusalem that connects the city with the village of Bethany, home of Lazarus, Mary and Martha, which became a retreat for Jesus from the hustle and bustle of the city streets. Nowadays it is the place where many pilgrimages to Jerusalem begin: it is possible to walk down its slopes to the garden of Gethsemane, along its winding, tarmacked, single-track road, and many pilgrim groups do this, singing and waving palm branches. At the top is the church of Dominus Flevit, 'The Lord wept', which is dedicated to the story of Jesus weeping over Jerusalem in Luke 19:41.

Run by the Franciscans, Dominus Flevit is a modern church built by Antonio Barluzzi in the mid 1950s. On the outside, perched on its upper levels where you might expect to see gargoyles, are some small vases, one on each corner of the tower. These are lachrymatories—jars for collecting tears—and the whole grey-domed church is meant to look like a teardrop. Many groups pray in this church before reliving the Palm Sunday procession, recalling how Jesus entered the city in humility, weeping first and then descending on a donkey rather than in regal power (see Matthew 21:1–11). There is a symbolic connection with King David, who went up the Mount of Olives weeping after running away from his son Absalom (2 Samuel 15:30).

The Mount of Olives is a place of tears and of hope. It is associated with Jesus both going down and going up; it has significance for his coming and his going. He arrives in humble glory on what we now call Palm Sunday, with only a few days of normal life left to him, and he departs 40 days after his Easter rising, commissioning his newly converted followers as ministers, witnesses and evangelists of the good news of salvation. Yet Jesus had walked up and down that gentle mountain many times before; he would have known its turns and bumps like the back of his hand. It was a special route and a tedious walk, yet it was not very far. Judaism had originally forbidden walking on the sabbath day ('Each of you stay where you are; do not leave your place on the seventh day', Exodus 16:29), but, before the time of Jesus, rabbis had modified the law to permit a distance of up to 2000 cubits, interpreting Joshua 3:4–5 as allowing some travel. By Jesus' time, the Pharisees had doubled the allowance: since a cubit is about 18 inches, a distance of about a mile was permitted. Soon they doubled it again, in order to permit both going and coming back. Jesus' comings and goings on the Mount of Olives were not in defiance of Jewish law, even though he often criticised the Pharisees for behaving as though humanity was made for the sabbath rather then vice versa.

As we journey backwards through the life and ministry of Jesus, we soon find ourselves at the Mount of Olives, whose association with the ascension is often overlooked. There is, however, a small chapel dedicated to the ascension to be found. Helena, mother of the Emperor Constantine, picked out two sites of significance on the Mount of Olives around AD326–328, and today one can still visit the Chapel of the Ascension and a cave where the Lord's Prayer was supposedly first taught. The latter, now the Church of the Paternoster, is a beautiful place, where the Lord's Prayer is on display in just about every known language. Whether Jesus really did teach the Lord's Prayer at this ancient site is a moot point, but it is another moment in his ministry to add to Palm

Sunday and the ascension, giving the Mount of Olives even more significance for pilgrims. The Chapel of the Ascension itself is not often visited: it is now a mosque, and its claim to house the rock from which Jesus actually ascended, in which is imprinted his footprint, is surely spurious.

The Mount of Olives has always been sacred to Judaism. Many Jews seek to be buried on its slopes, overlooking Jerusalem, because of a tradition derived from Zechariah 14:4 that the resurrection will begin on the Mount. Accordingly there is now an extensive graveyard overlooking the city, the view from which is, perhaps ironically, dominated by the Islamic golden Dome of the Rock, itself revered as a site of ascension—that of the prophet Mohammed.

So one site of ascension looks down on another across a city of faith and ferment. Three Abrahamic religions live cheek by jowl, with much in common and much to fight over. Their sites of pilgrimage draw thousands of tourists and pilgrims annually, although the Christian population of Jerusalem is now minuscule, having been squeezed out by Jews and Muslims, among whom the city is geographically divided, east and west. Perhaps one day it will be possible to rise above the conflicts and competition that have marred and marked the history of Jerusalem, whose peace and prosperity are still very much a focus for prayer today.

Lord, though parted from our sight, alleluia,
far above the starry height, alleluia,
grant our hearts may thither rise, alleluia,
seeking thee above the skies. Alleluia.

CHARLES WESLEY (1707–88)

10 December

Going fishing on the sea of Galilee

After these things Jesus showed himself again to the disciples by the Sea of Tiberias; and he showed himself in this way... When they had gone ashore, they saw a charcoal fire there, with fish on it, and bread. Jesus said to them, 'Bring some of the fish that you have just caught.' So Simon Peter went aboard and hauled the net ashore, full of large fish, a hundred and fifty-three of them; and though there were so many, the net was not torn. Jesus said to them, 'Come and have breakfast.' Now none of the disciples dared to ask him, 'Who are you?' because they knew it was the Lord. Jesus came and took the bread and gave it to them, and did the same with the fish. This was now the third time that Jesus appeared to the disciples after he was raised from the dead.

JOHN 21:1, 9–14

The Sea of Galilee is one of the most authentic sites in the Holy Land. Also known as Lake Tiberias or the Lake of Gennesaret, it is basically unchanged since biblical times, so a trip on the lake can be both a very pleasant and a profound experience. If a storm suddenly brews up, one can have a very real sense of what it might have been like for the fishermen disciples, whose lives and livelihood revolved around this vital expanse of fresh water.

The lowest freshwater lake on earth, Galilee is fed by underground springs and the River Jordan, which effectively flows through it. In Jesus' time it was surrounded by fishing villages and is associated with famous miracles such as the walking on the water (Matthew 14:22–33) and the calming of the storm (Mark 4:35–41). The multiplication of the loaves and fishes (Mark 6:30–46) and this post-resurrection appearance of Jesus are associated specifically with Tabgha, while nearby at Genessaret (Ginosar), a 2000-year-old fishing boat, dug up from the silt, can be viewed at the Beit Yigal Allon Museum. Known as the 'Jesus boat', it is a carefully preserved physical object that connects us to the time and place of Christ and his disciples.

The town of Tiberias was the newly founded capital of the Roman 'tetrarchy' ruled by Herod Antipas, who named it after the emperor Tiberius (42BC–AD37). Herod Antipas was one of three sons of the tyrant Herod the Great, who was ruling when Jesus was born. His kingdom was then divided, under Roman authority, among Antipas, Archelaus and Philip. Archelaus got Judea, Philip got the east side of the Jordan and Antipas got Galilee and Perea. He built Tiberias in AD20, and today it has added tourism to its ancient role as a fishing village.

The lake mirrors the events and locations of Jesus' ministry. On the shoreline at Tabgha is the Church of the Primacy of St Peter, which commemorates the episode immediately after the breakfast on the beach, when Jesus asks Peter three times if he loves him and then tells him to feed the flock, thereby reasserting Peter as the senior disciple on whose rocklike faith the Church will be established. Built in 1933, the Church of the Primacy has within it a chalkstone table (*Mensa Christi*) on which, tradition has it, Jesus actually ate breakfast with the disciples. We do not have to commit wholesale to the authenticity of this rock table; we might prefer simply to stand on the shoreline and recall the story, reflecting on the passage of time and the fact that we are standing on the very same shore, looking at the same water. For many, this is just as edifying, if not more so, as entering a church erected on top of a site that was identified by an early pilgrim or an enthusiastic Pope. Many pilgrimage groups, therefore, like to celebrate Holy Communion on a simple altar built close to the water, in the open air. With no buildings in sight, the simpler truths can come to the fore.

It is indeed true that, over the centuries, Christians have encrusted the faith with a lot of paraphernalia. It is hard nowadays to consider the events of Jesus' life and ministry at face value. In this story, we are told that the disciples, who have returned to work after the harrowing events of the crucifixion, see Jesus on the shore. They are having no luck catching fish, so, at his suggestion, they cast their nets on the other side of the boat. It is a simple technique, by which weighted nets are thrown overboard and the movement of the boat, blown by the wind, drags them through the water, trawling whatever is in their path. Jesus' advice is good, and they haul ashore 153 fish to add to those that Jesus is already cooking for them. It is the first Christian 'bring and share' meal!

Many scholars have discussed the significance of the 153 fish. St Jerome (c.347–420) first suggested that there were 153 species of fish known at the time. However, we cannot be sure that this is true. Some, assuming that John is making a theological rather than historical point in writing the story, have extrapolated that it is a veiled reference to the number of the nations: if every type of fish fits in the net, then every type of person can be caught for Christ. Others have suggested that the Torah, when read in the synagogue at the time of Jesus, was subdivided into 153 parts. St Augustine remembered that 153 is the 17th triangular number (17+16+15... +3+2+1=153), and rather liked the idea that there are ten commandments and seven gifts of the Spirit, thereby combining divine grace with the law. We can take our pick of these suggestions and might wonder whether it matters, over and above the simple possibility that John tells us there were 153 fish because there were 153 fish! He was there at the time, after all, and, as professional fishermen, the disciples would have counted them and sold the ones they did not eat themselves.

As we inch along on our backward journey, travelling not only in time but into the Holy Land itself, where so much is invested in the significance of place, it can be useful to remember what we are looking for. Holy sites ground these holy stories in reality, but we are tracing the significance of Jesus himself and the meaning of his life and work for the salvation of humankind.

In simple trust like theirs who heard,
beside the Syrian sea,
the gracious calling of the Lord,
let us, like them, without a word,
rise up and follow thee.
JOHN WHITTIER (1807–92)

11 December

Going to Emmaus

Now on that same day two of them were going to a village called Emmaus, about seven miles from Jerusalem, and talking with each other about all these things that had happened. While they were talking and discussing, Jesus himself came near and went with them, but their eyes were kept from recognising him. And he said to them, 'What are you discussing with each other while you walk along?' They stood still, looking sad. Then one of them, whose name was Cleopas, answered him, 'Are you the only stranger in Jerusalem who does not know the things that have taken place there in these days?' He asked them, 'What things?' They replied, 'The things about Jesus of Nazareth, who was a prophet mighty in deed and word before God and all the people, and how our chief priests and leaders handed him over to be condemned to death and crucified him. But we had hoped that he was the one to redeem Israel...' Then he said to them, 'Oh, how foolish you are, and how slow of heart to believe all that the prophets have declared! Was it not necessary that the Messiah should suffer these things and then enter into his glory?' Then beginning with Moses and all the prophets, he interpreted to them the things about himself in all the scriptures.

As they came near the village to which they were going, he walked ahead as if he were going on. But they urged him strongly, saying, 'Stay with us, because it is almost evening and the day is now nearly over.' So he went in to stay with them. When he was at the table with them, he took bread, blessed and broke it, and gave it to them. Then their eyes were opened, and they recognised him; and he vanished from their sight. They said to each other, 'Were not our hearts burning within us while he was talking to us on the road, while he was opening the scriptures to us?'

LUKE 24:13–21A, 25–33

Where is Emmaus? No one knows for sure. Some recent scholarship has suggested that there was no place with that name, and that we have arrived at 'Emmaus' as a truncation of the word 'Oulammaus'. In the Greek version of the Old Testament (the Septuagint), this is the name of the place (now known as Luz) where Jacob dreamt of angels on a ladder going up and down to heaven (Genesis 28:10–19). The Codex Bezae Cantabrigiensis, a fifth-century Greek New Testament manuscript now held in Cambridge, uniquely refers to the place of Jesus' appearance to Cleopas and his companion as 'Oulammaus', along with many other small textual variations. Although there is a mistake of translation built into this connection, it was unidentified in the first century, and this use of 'Oulammaus' would link the two stories nicely (Jesus appears to the two disciples at the place where God revealed himself to Jacob). There is therefore a view that the story emphasises this throwback to Jacob, and that there need not be a place called Emmaus at all.

This does not mean that the encounter did not happen or, indeed, that the village cannot be identified. We are told the location of Bethany (in John 11:18), and Luke tells us that Emmaus is about three times as far away (60 stadia or 10–12 kilometres), although he fails to mention in which direction. Consequently there have been various identifications of the village where Jesus broke bread with his followers (thus celebrating the first post-resurrection Holy Communion). The earliest comes from Eusebius, who identified a place called Emmaus Nicopolis in the third century. When Jerome translated his work, he led posterity to believe that there was a church there, built on Cleopas' house. This ancient identification spawned the idea, 700 years later, that there could be a useful place of pilgrimage midway between Jerusalem and Emmaus Nicopolis, so the Crusaders built a church on the Kiryat Anavim road, now known as Abu Ghosh. If Emmaus Nicopolis was the village where Cleopas lived, and where he invited Jesus to his house to eat and 'abide with them', then there must have been a particular place along the road where the risen Christ met them and walked.

The church of Abu Ghosh is very much open to visitors and is a very beautiful, serene place. Many pilgrimage groups celebrate the Eucharist there, and, while the site may not have a watertight claim to authenticity, it has come to represent Emmaus and its wonderful story of casual conversation between the risen Christ and downcast disciples, who recognised him only in the breaking of bread. Originally built in 1140 and destroyed in 1187, the church was rebuilt and is now run by the Lazarist Fathers, who extend a peaceful and profound welcome. The church also has a fabulous acoustic for singing.

Emmaus could have been anywhere; it would hardly matter. Cleopas' companion is not given a name, and we might draw significance from this: his companion is Everyman—that is, you or I. We are on that road, and countless others have walked it before us. For 2000 years the church has called, ordained and educated men and women to represent Christ on the roads of our lives and to break bread, remembering his call to 'do this in remembrance of me'. Through them the church has invited everyone to partake in a communion that is as much about companionship on the road as it is about consuming and becoming the body of Christ. The word 'companion' is derived from the Latin *com* ('with') and *pane* ('bread'). So, as companions on the way of Christ, we are truly those who walk together and break bread together. That is what 'companionship' means.

Furthermore, the story reminds us that built into Christian companionship is the remembering and exposition of scripture, too. Cleopas and Everyman needed to have the story explained from both ends, as it were. They knew their Jewish scriptures, but Jesus needed to explain that those scriptures all pointed to him. When he had done so, everything fell into place and the scales fell from their eyes. It was a magical moment, a spiritual equivalent of a 'eureka!' moment. John Wesley famously described his conversion as like having his 'heart strangely warmed'. In this story, word and sacrament combine to reveal the presence of Christ, Word made flesh and flesh made bread in one all-converting experience. No wonder their hearts burned within them!

O thou who camest from above,
The pure celestial fire to impart,
Kindle a flame of sacred love
On the mean altar of my heart.
CHARLES WESLEY (1707–88)

12 December

Coming out of the garden tomb

On the first day of the week, at early dawn, they came to the tomb, taking the spices that they had prepared. They found the stone rolled away from the tomb, but when they went in, they did not find the body. While they were perplexed about this, suddenly two men in dazzling clothes stood beside them. The women were terrified and bowed their faces to the ground, but the men said to them, 'Why do you look for the living among the dead? He is not here, but has risen. Remember how he told you, while he was still in Galilee, that the Son of Man must be handed over to sinners, and be crucified, and on the third day rise again.' Then they remembered his words, and returning from the tomb, they told all this to the eleven and to all the rest. Now it was Mary Magdalene, Joanna, Mary the mother of James, and the other women with them who told this to the apostles. But these words seemed to them an idle tale, and they did not believe them. But Peter got up and ran to the tomb; stooping and looking in, he saw the linen cloths by themselves; then he went home, amazed at what had happened.

LUKE 24:1–12

In Jerusalem today there are two sites laying claim to be the site of the resurrection. Near a bus station, on the edge of an escarpment, there is a rock formation that, given the right light and angle, does look very much like a skull-shaped rock. For many pilgrims, this evocation of the site of crucifixion and the resonance with the Gospel writers' location of Calvary at Golgotha (the 'place of the skull') is powerful and moving. Identified as such in 1842 and endorsed as authentic by General Charles Gordon in 1883, the belief that it might be the site of Jesus' death on the cross was bolstered in 1867 by the discovery of a tomb in a location that could have been the garden owned by Joseph of Arimathea. Ever since, that site has been a place of pilgrimage, not in opposition to the ancient traditional location of Calvary at the Church of the Holy Sepulchre, but in addition to it.

The Garden Tomb does not carry the weight of history, as the Church of the Holy Sepulchre does. Indeed, the weathered rockface that today resembles a skull may not have looked so, 2000 years ago. Its claim to authenticity is weaker, yet it provokes neither the hustle and bustle of sharp-elbowed pilgrimage nor the impatient queuing or wholesale candle lighting. Nor does it host the competing religious ceremonies in different languages, which barely conceal the unecumenical intolerance that exists between Orthodox and Armenian congregations who share the more ancient site. To that extent, the Church of the Holy Sepulchre reflects the upheavals not only of Jesus' times, but also of our own. In contrast, the Garden Tomb maintains a peaceful, beautiful garden environment, offering an evangelistic guided tour that culminates in a tomb that looks authentic, into which one can walk and look around without being pestered or nudged out of the way.

The Garden Tomb is a wonderfully serene place to visit, to pause, pray and rest. One can talk to companions or seek solitude, and the ambience of tranquillity is very conducive to personal reflection. In our busy world, where silence is golden and contemplation rare, the ability to do this is a gift indeed. Jesus' death on the cross happened in the middle of a muddle of noise—shouting, weeping, screaming, nailing, howling, thunder and lightning as the heavens were torn and the Son of God met an inhumane end. The crescendo of anger, dishonesty, injustice and brutality climaxed with hammer blows on the anvil of incarnation, and then all was silence. At last, when the clamour had died with the man, the silence of the grave held the tension of the unresolved chord of anticipation until, in the silence of Easter morning, the tomb emptied and victory was won.

The relationship between the cross and the resurrection is almost musical. As in a piece of music, the discordance of crucifixion—very much in a minor key, if you will—sets up a tension that resolves into the sunny major harmonies of Easter's resurrection morning. It is familiar music: like the Good Friday hymns that we always sing, we know our way around and we know what comes next. The crucifixion and resurrection complement each other, and the agonising tensions of the cross are bearable because we know how they will resolve. Music pushes on to resolution: it needs to resolve, and we can feel it when it does. We can hear and bear the discordance and incompleteness, because we know that resolution, completeness and concord will surely follow, just as Easter follows Good Friday. If we go to church on Good Friday, we have to go on Easter Sunday too, otherwise it doesn't add up, and we are left with a sense of incompleteness, suspended between death and life.

Whenever we place ourselves at the foot of the cross, as we and countless millions may have done many times over the last 2000 years, it is the same every time. And yet it is different every time, because each one of us, and the world we inhabit, changes. The juxtaposition of the cross and the world is different every time they meet, every time they intersect, every time they *cross*. The cross gives a repetitive but fresh perspective on the affairs of the world and on the details of our own life and faith, because it is an unchanging statement of God's love for the world. It is a love involving huge sacrifice and cost, purchasing the greatest gift of salvation. It is exactly the same when we bring the hope of resurrection into play, for while the cross casts its shadow over every news bulletin we hear, the same news is illuminated with resurrection light. We cannot have one without the other, and that is why there is always hope.

In their own way—through their location, aspect, history and spirituality—each of these two sites of the resurrection has something profound to reveal to us (and any pilgrim should visit both). One is noisy and busy, the other quiet and peaceful. Each has its own validity. Although both are empty tombs, what is most significant is not that they are tombs but that they are empty. They are both sites of resurrection, and, because Christ has left his tomb empty, resurrection is opened up for any and all of us, in any place, in any age.

> *Good Joseph had a garden,*
> *Close by that sad green hill*
> *Where Jesus died a bitter death*
> *To save mankind from ill.*
> ALDA M. MILNER-BARRY (1875–1940)

13 December

Coming to the cross at Calvary

Two others also, who were criminals, were led away to be put to death with him. When they came to the place that is called The Skull, they crucified Jesus there with the criminals, one on his right and one on his left. Then Jesus said, 'Father, forgive them; for they do not know what they are doing. And they cast lots to divide his clothing... It was now about noon, and darkness came over the whole land until three in the afternoon, while the sun's light failed; and the curtain of the temple was torn in two. Then Jesus, crying with a loud voice, said, 'Father, into your hands I commend my spirit.' Having said this, he breathed his last... Now there was a good and righteous man named Joseph, who, though a member of the council, had not agreed to their plan and action. He came from the Jewish town of Arimathea, and he was waiting expectantly for the kingdom of God. This man went to Pilate and asked for the body of Jesus. Then he took it down, wrapped it in a linen cloth, and laid it in a rock-hewn tomb where no one had ever been laid.

LUKE 23:32–34, 44–46, 50–53

Yesterday we took a look at the Garden Tomb site in Jerusalem. The Church of the Holy Sepulchre has a much longer heritage and tradition and has been venerated as the authentic site of Golgotha since Eusebius identified it in the early second century. Around 325, the first Christian Roman Emperor, Constantine, replaced a pagan temple on the site with a church, and it wasn't long before his mother, Helena, claimed to have found the true cross, and a grave. This is the reason that the church there still has a double function: it is believed to be the site both of Calvary and of the tomb that Joseph gave for Jesus' burial. The church building encompasses two places of pilgrimage—a rocky outcrop on which the cross is supposed to have stood and a construction within the church, about 100 metres away, where a rock tomb was cut away to create a kind of shrine, into which half a dozen people can enter to pray.

Nowadays there can be long queues to visit these two sacred spaces. First, the pilgrims ascend to an upper level and kneel at the site of crucifixion, placing a hand through an opening in the floor in order to touch the piece of rock that supposedly housed the base of the cross. Whether the rock is authentic or not, millions of people have been doing this for hundreds of years, so it is a place where 'prayer has been valid' (T.S. Eliot) for centuries, where curiosity or tourism gives way to a profound sense of sacred space.

Visitors then descend to a slab on which it is said that Jesus' body was laid out in preparation for burial. Many people place objects on the slab to 'absorb' something of the holiness that it exudes. This practice does not appeal to everyone, but there is true devotion to be found here, at any time. Another very short walk around a corner leads to the wooden structure around the tomb. Unless it is very early on a Sunday morning, there are long queues to visit this small but hugely significant dark place from which the Saviour of the world emerged in resurrection light.

However devout or credulous the pilgrims are, the Holy Sepulchre church is a pilgrimage site *par excellence*. Firstly, it has a claim to be authentic: any debate about the exact location of the site of crucifixion must begin with the real possibility that Eusebius, Constantine and Helena got it right. Secondly, the site has been visited, venerated and vilified for 1800 years. Thirdly, it has been damaged, desecrated, defiled and rebuilt in response to religious wars, political arguments and ecumenical arguments. The tomb itself has had death and resurrection experiences of its own. Currently a safe place to visit, it holds together its own history with the tensions and troubles of modern Jerusalem, while remaining rooted in the core events and beliefs of the most significant religion the planet has known.

The Church of the Holy Sepulchre evokes the crucifixion more than the resurrection. The Garden Tomb around the corner focuses visitors on resurrection rather than crucifixion. They complement one another. The desire to find a more authentic site, manifested in General Gordon's affirmation of the Garden Tomb as a more 'Protestant' destination for pilgrimage, reveals not an 'either–or' dilemma (about which is the more authentic) but, rather, a 'both–and' paradox. Each site has something to say to us and do for us. We need them both, to represent the agony of crucifixion followed by the restorative joy of resurrection. The Church of the Holy Sepulchre sets up tensions that can be resolved in the Garden Tomb. As a site of prayer and history, the Holy Sepulchre raises questions about where God is to be found in the midst of extreme outward devotion, sacred objects, relics and the clamour of pushing and shoving, against a background of competing masses and liturgies. Where is the man of Galilee in this, and where is his heavenly Father to be found in the trappings of established, perhaps even superstitious faith? These are relevant but, perhaps, edgy questions to ask of one of the most sacred sites in the world.

Yet, if the site of death and resurrection is a place for edginess and challenging questions, nothing could be more appropriate, for the death and resurrection of Christ—literally the crux of God's divine plan for incarnation and salvation—lies at the heart of every aspect of faith. No one can doubt that Christ lived and died. It is a brave and radical historian who will argue that Jesus' crucifixion is a fiction (writers who had no apostolic faith testify to it). Most important, though, is the significance of that death.

Why did Jesus die? And did he rise from the dead? These are the key questions, which must be, and are, asked even in the midst of the hustle and bustle of a pilgrimage site erected not only to present the truth of these claims but also to promote devotion to them. While the Holy Sepulchre asks these questions, it is at the Garden Tomb that we might find the answers. In musical terms, the dominant church raises tensions that are resolved in the healthy, uncluttered tonic of the Garden Tomb, for after the clamour comes the need to step away and reflect, consider the evidence, pray, and ultimately admit that while the mysteries of resurrection and salvation are ours to ponder and marvel at, they are not ours to solve.

In life, no house, no home
My Lord on earth might have;
In death, no friendly tomb,
But what a stranger gave.
What may I say?
Heav'n was his home;
But mine the tomb
Wherein he lay.

SAMUEL CROSSMAN (C.1624–83)

14 December

Going out for a last supper

Then came the day of Unleavened Bread, on which the Passover lamb had to be sacrificed. So Jesus sent Peter and John, saying, 'Go and prepare the Passover meal for us that we may eat it.' They asked him, 'Where do you want us to make preparations for it?' 'Listen,' he said to them, 'when you have entered the city, a man carrying a jar of water will meet you; follow him into the house he enters and say to the owner of the house, 'The teacher asks you, "Where is the guest room, where I may eat the Passover with my disciples?" He will show you a large room upstairs, already furnished. Make preparations for us there.' So they went and found everything as he had told them; and they prepared the Passover meal. When the hour came, he took his place at the table, and the apostles with him. He said to them, 'I have eagerly desired to eat this Passover with you before I suffer; for I tell you, I will not eat it until it is fulfilled in the kingdom of God.' Then he took a cup, and after giving thanks he said, 'Take this and divide it among yourselves; for I tell you that from now on I will not drink of the fruit of the vine until the kingdom of God comes.' Then he took a loaf of bread, and when he had given thanks, he broke it and gave it to them, saying, 'This is my body, which is given for you. Do this in remembrance of me.' And he did the same with the cup after supper, saying, 'This cup that is poured out for you is the new covenant in my blood.

LUKE 22:7–20

In our reverse pilgrimage, we have been to the upper room before (see 8 December), and now we return to see it for the first time. Known as the Cenacle or *Cenaculum* (because *cena*, in Latin, means 'evening meal'), it is the room in which the last supper and the foot-washing are supposed to have taken place. It is also the room associated with the descent of the Holy Spirit at Pentecost, and various other post-resurrection appearances. With verbal irony, the first time we visit the room is at the last supper, and thereafter it becomes a kind of safe and sacred place for the apostles. They retreat to it after the crucifixion, to hide; Jesus reveals himself there to Thomas and also breathes on them the Holy Spirit (John 20:19–29). Later, in the same room, they elect Matthias to succeed the traitor Judas (Acts 1:15–26). Thus there is a connection, in this place, between Jesus' self-sacrifice and his mission—a connection between his physical, bodily suffering and the spiritual outpouring that follows the resurrection. Wherever and whatever the upper room was, it is a very significant place.

Traditional pilgrimage has located the upper room on Mount Zion in the centre of Jerusalem, and the early pilgrim Egeria visited the site in 384. She was probably a nun from northern Spain (Galicia) who visited Palestine and kept a journal of her discoveries and experiences. The journal, as well as giving us insights into the early supposed locations of some of the sites of significant events in the life of Christ, describes in detail the liturgical practices that Egeria encountered. Her writings are therefore very helpful to scholars of early liturgy, particularly concerning the manner in which Holy Communion was celebrated in the first few centuries after Jesus instituted it at a Passover supper in the upper room.

The last supper is a pivotal event in history—an ending and a beginning. No Passover had ever been like it before, and none would or could be the same thereafter. As a Jew, Jesus' plan to celebrate the Passover with his friends, and his instruction to Peter and John to meet a man who would take them to the upstairs guest room in his house, are not remarkable at all. Many houses had 'upper' rooms: they were built atop the flat roof of a typical Hebrew house. Sometimes the upper room was on a third storey: in Acts 20:8–9, when Eutychus fell out of a window while Paul was speaking, he fell three storeys. Upper rooms are dangerous places, precariously placed between the realms of life and death. King Ahaziah also had a fatal fall from an upper room (2 Kings 1:2), but did not have anyone to raise him back to life. Elijah carried the widow of Zarephath's son to an upper room to raise him (1 Kings 17:19–23), and David went to one to mourn Absalom (2 Samuel 18:33). Dorcas was taken to an upper room when she died, and Peter went up to her to pray for her restoration (Acts 9:36–41).

The last supper, then, takes place in a room that is poised between life and death. It is also a room with a view—a view across the rooftops of Jerusalem, for sure, but also a view across the past and future of Jewish and Christian faith. The last supper is a vantage point from which to look forwards and backwards nearly 2000 years in each direction. From our viewpoint, 2000 years ahead, we can see how the exodus of the Israelites from Egypt ultimately led to the moment when Jesus said, 'This is my body, this is my blood; do this in remembrance of me.' Every celebration of the Eucharist since has looked back to that moment when Christ commanded us to re-member him in bread and wine. We do not dis-member him—break him apart and scatter his story in pieces like a broken chandelier. Rather, we re-member him: we piece together, each and every time, the saving unity of his words and actions by which we ourselves are his body on earth, not just *telling* his saving love, but *being* it.

As we remember the last supper, we are not only transported to that upper room, to be with Christ, but we are transported beyond it, back to the original Passover, when the Israelites fled Egypt with their sandals untied and their bread undercooked. At the heart of that event was the sacrifice of the lamb, whose blood marked the wooden doorposts of those who were to be saved. A millennium-and-a-half later, it was Jesus who, as the remembrance of the first Passover was being enacted in Jerusalem, declared himself to be the true sacrifice of God. His blood spilled down the wood of the cross so that not only the Jewish nation but the whole world might be saved from sin and death through the power of something as yet unseen and unheard—the resurrection. The Israelites could not see that as they fled Egypt, and Jesus' disciples could not see it as he broke bread and drank wine with them, describing himself as the Passover Lamb. Yet we can, as we survey the landscape of salvation history from our third-millennium vantage point, and we re-member him in bread and wine still.

> That last night, at supper lying,
> 'mid the Twelve, his chosen band,
> Jesus, with the law complying,
> keeps the feast its rites demand;
> then, more precious food supplying,
> gives himself with his own hand.
>
> THOMAS AQUINAS (C.1225–74)

15 December

Lazarus, come out!

When Jesus arrived, he found that Lazarus had already been in the tomb for four days. Now Bethany was near Jerusalem, some two miles away, and many of the Jews had come to Martha and Mary to console them about their brother. When Martha heard that Jesus was coming, she went and met him, while Mary stayed at home. Martha said to Jesus, 'Lord, if you had been here, my brother would not have died. But even now I know that God will give you whatever you ask of him.' Jesus said to her, 'Your brother will rise again.' Martha said to him, 'I know that he will rise again in the resurrection on the last day.' Jesus said to her, 'I am the resurrection and the life. Those who believe in me, even though they die, will live, and everyone who lives and believes in me will never die.'...

Then Jesus, again greatly disturbed, came to the tomb. It was a cave, and a stone was lying against it. Jesus said, 'Take away the stone.' Martha, the sister of the dead man, said to him, 'Lord, already there is a stench because he has been dead for four days.' Jesus said to her, 'Did I not tell you that if you believed, you would see the glory of God?' So they took away the stone. And Jesus looked upwards and said, 'Father, I thank you for having heard me. I knew that you always hear me, but I have said this for the sake of the crowd standing here, so that they may believe that you sent me.' When he had said this, he cried with a loud voice, 'Lazarus, come out!' The dead man came out, his hands and feet bound with strips

of cloth, and his face wrapped in a cloth. Jesus said to them,
'Unbind him, and let him go.'

JOHN 11:17–26, 38–44

The raising of Lazarus is one of the most fantastical stories
in the New Testament, yet it is grounded in real people and
places, and a visit to Palestine today brings the conjunction of
the normal and the supernatural into sharp relief. Our faith is
sharpened as we relate biblical stories to modern geography
and politics.

Mary, Martha and Lazarus were a family, three siblings
who lived together in Bethany, on the eastern slopes of the
Mount of Olives, within walking distance of Jerusalem. Also
in Bethany lived Simon the leper, in whose house Jesus was
anointed with oil by an unnamed woman (Matthew 26:6–
13), and one of Jesus' final appearances to the disciples took
place in the town (Luke 24:50). In John's Gospel (12:1–3),
Mary is identified as the one who anoints Jesus' feet in
Bethany. If it could be said that Jesus had a 'family' to be
with and a 'base' while in Jerusalem, the home of Mary,
Martha and Lazarus and the village of Bethany best qualify.

Bethany is not to be confused with Bethany beyond
the Jordan, where John the Baptist baptised (John 1:28).
Similarly, Lazarus of Bethany, Jesus' friend, is not to be
confused with the Lazarus of the parable in Luke 16:19–31,
a representative figure whose piety and suffering are used as
a foil to the arrogance of wealth (see 4 December). However,
for both characters, the meaning of Lazarus, 'God is my
helper', is more than apposite.

Another version of the name is Eleazar, and the modern
name of Bethany is al-Eizariya, 'the 'place of Lazarus'.
Although this village was inhabited for about 600 years

before Jesus went there, it has become known as Lazarus' village because of a popular tradition that connected the person and place. That tradition has survived hundreds of years, such that now 'the tomb of Lazarus' is a popular destination for pilgrims.

Whether the humble cave now signposted as Lazarus' tomb really was the place or not is questionable; less so is the tradition that locates it, and the village of Bethany, in an area that was a first-century graveyard, identified as significant since the fourth century. Muslims and Christians have venerated the site for centuries, and now it is situated in the West Bank Palestinian territory of the modern Holy Land. In the 13th century the al-Uzair mosque was built there. It was expanded by the Ottomans in the 16th century, and Christians worshipped in it for 100 years before church authorities forbade the practice.

There is no more powerful a symbol of resurrection than an empty tomb. Lazarus' tomb, like Jesus', is empty. The Christian era has seen the establishment of many shrines— elaborate graves containing relics of saints, the presence of whose very bones inspired pilgrims centuries ago and, to some extent, still does. But the empty tomb in the Church of the Holy Sepulchre, and the Garden Tomb, and, indeed, the tomb of Lazarus at al-Eizariya not only testify to the actual resurrections that took place there or nearby, but are also powerful reminders of the resurrection offered to us all after our earthly life is over.

Reading backwards, we encountered Jesus' resurrection before the raising of Lazarus. This reminds us that Jesus' resurrection is a prerequisite of Lazarus'. It would be wrong to say that Lazarus' resurrection, coming first chronologically, makes Christ's possible. Rather, it is Christ's resurrection, to follow, that makes Lazarus' possible. Because Christ *will* be raised, Lazarus *was* raised. Lazarus' raising prefigures Jesus' resurrection, but, as soon as Christ is raised, it takes on different power and meaning. Only after Jesus' resurrection does Lazarus' make sense: it both points to and is dependent on Jesus'. In telling the story in his central, eleventh chapter, John knows what will come in his 20th, and he knows that we do too. In his Gospel it is as though everything is happening at once and can be told in any order, because, in the bigger picture of incarnation, ministry, death and resurrection, all things hang and hold together. They can be viewed from any angle, like a three-dimensional glass jigsaw, in which all the pieces reflect each other—and the light they give off, separately and collectively, is the resurrection light of Christ.

Now is eternal life,
if ris'n with Christ we stand,
in him to life reborn,
and held within his hand;
No more we fear death's ancient dread,
in Christ arisen from the dead.
GEORGE WALLACE BRIGGS (1875–1959)

16 December

Going up Mount Tabor

Jesus took with him Peter and James and his brother John and led them up a high mountain, by themselves. And he was transfigured before them, and his face shone like the sun, and his clothes became dazzling white. Suddenly there appeared to them Moses and Elijah, talking with him. Then Peter said to Jesus, 'Lord, it is good for us to be here; if you wish, I will make three dwellings here, one for you, one for Moses, and one for Elijah.' While he was still speaking, suddenly a bright cloud overshadowed them, and from the cloud a voice said, 'This is my Son, the Beloved; with him I am well pleased; listen to him!' When the disciples heard this, they fell to the ground and were overcome by fear. But Jesus came and touched them, saying, 'Get up and do not be afraid.' And when they looked up, they saw no one except Jesus himself alone.

MATTHEW 17:1–8

There are two candidates for the location of this pivotal event in the Gospels. The traditional location, identified by Origen in the third century and St Cyril of Jerusalem and St Jerome in the fourth century, is Mount Tabor, and the Church of the Transfiguration can be found on top of that mountain, welcoming pilgrims today. More recently, the theologians Joseph B. Lightfoot and Daniel Fuller suggested (in the 17th and 20th centuries respectively) that the transfiguration might have occurred on top of Mount Hermon, as it is higher than Tabor and nearer to Caesarea Philippi, which is where the immediately preceding narratives take place. Nevertheless, tradition and popular piety favour Mount Tabor.

Mount Tabor is 1886 feet (575 metres) high and rises above the surrounding plains in an imposing manner. The church on top of it is visible from the ground and, by the same token, commands fantastic views for anyone who goes up to it. Ascending is something of an adventure. It is no longer necessary to climb 4340 steps or walk up a winding track, but tourist buses now drive up to a certain height; then there is a car parking area from which local minibuses take visitors and pilgrims up the remaining single-track road to the summit. These minibuses are a relatively recent development: until recently, taxi drivers raced up and down round the hairpin bends, one of whom, notoriously, had only one arm.

Nowadays it takes perhaps a little less faith to go to the top, which is an oasis of calm, run by Italian Franciscans, who also serve an excellent cappuccino (free to priests!). The church itself is relatively modern, built between 1919 and 1924 by the Italian architect Barluzzi. Previously, there had been a Crusader church since the twelfth century and a Byzantine one from the fifth or sixth century. The site has therefore been revered as the site of the transfiguration for over 1500 years.

Mount Tabor is a vantage point in every sense of the word. From its summit, we can not only see literally for miles; we can also look forwards and backwards in time. Armageddon, the place where the final battle will take place (Revelation 16:16), lies at the foot of the mountain. The story of Jesus being seen on the mountain, dazzling white, with Moses and Elijah in attendance, occurs midway through the Gospels, and we are reading it almost halfway through this journey backwards through the Bible. The transfiguration is a central point in Jesus' ministry, and it points us backwards to the prophecies of the Old Testament and forwards to the radical changes to be brought about in his passion, death and resurrection. Here, on the mount of transfiguration, these points intersect and connect.

Astronomers tell us that, as we look far out into space, we are looking further back in time. A speck of light from a source that is 1000 light years away has taken 1000 years to reach our eyes, so we are looking at something that occurred 1000 years ago. Scientists are getting closer to looking back at, even recreating, the experience of the Big Bang, 13.8 billion years ago. Space and time are connected irrevocably, and, over great distances, can even be considered as inseparable.

So what were Peter and James and John seeing? On one level they were witnessing a break in space and time, such that Moses, Elijah and Jesus occupied the same space. The laws of physics and history were bent, or warped. We know that Jesus, Moses and Elijah were not contemporaries, so the disciples were either imagining it or seeing some kind of trick, or it was an experience of a new, divine dimension. Whatever it was, it was also a representation of Jesus, the new covenant, alongside the pillars of the old covenant— the law (Moses) and the prophets (Elijah). There could be no better place than a high mountain to show this vantage point over the whole of divine and human history. During the experience, Jesus' form changed (which is what 'transfiguration' means). His body took on a glorious dimension—a foretaste of post-resurrection glory, perhaps, revealing what was yet to come. Past and future combine in the comings and goings on top of Tabor.

That this happened on planet earth 2000 years ago, witnessed by only a few but recorded for posterity, is, naturally, bewildering. It is unnatural, breaching accepted conventions of history, geography, time and space. It is a truly supernatural event, alongside the ascension and the resurrection. So, fantastical as it all may seem, when it comes to matters of faith, these are the zones we enter; these are the realms, beyond our own, of which we have a foretaste. These are the events that really matter, taking us beyond the nice idea that Jesus was a special person with good things to say, a moral code to promulgate and a way of life to teach us. Jesus is more than that. This story reminds us, as the voice of God is recorded as saying—there and then, here and now— 'This is my Son, the Beloved... listen to him.'

The transfiguration is a high-level, four-dimensional meeting of heaven and earth, a midpoint of Jesus' ministry, intersected by the past and the future, the human and the divine. After this there is no turning back. Jesus must descend to Jerusalem, to confront the authorities, preach the kingdom and face the inevitable and necessary consequences of human sin and divine incarnation. Jesus is on his own now: his cousin John has been beheaded, and he will soon raise Lazarus from the dead in another supernatural event that prefigures his own saving death and resurrection. We thought it had all begun. It has now.

'Tis good, Lord, to be here,
Thy beauty to behold,
Where Moses and Elijah stand,
Thy messengers of old.

Fulfiller of the past,
Promise of things to be,
We hail Thy body glorified
And our redemption see.

JOSEPH ARMITAGE ROBINSON (1858–1933)

John comes to grief at Machaerus

At that time Herod the ruler heard reports about Jesus; and he said to his servants, 'This is John the Baptist; he has been raised from the dead, and for this reason these powers are at work in him.' For Herod had arrested John, bound him, and put him in prison on account of Herodias, his brother Philip's wife, because John had been telling him, 'It is not lawful for you to have her.' Though Herod wanted to put him to death, he feared the crowd, because they regarded him as a prophet. But when Herod's birthday came, the daughter of Herodias danced before the company, and she pleased Herod so much that he promised on oath to grant her whatever she might ask. Prompted by her mother, she said, 'Give me the head of John the Baptist here on a platter.' The king was grieved, yet out of regard for his oaths and for the guests, he commanded it to be given; he sent and had John beheaded in the prison. The head was brought on a platter and given to the girl, who brought it to her mother. His disciples came and took the body and buried it; then they went and told Jesus.

MATTHEW 14:1–12

This tragic story starts in the wrong place. We are about to be told how John the Baptist was murdered by Herod Antipas, but this is not an account of the actual event; rather, it starts from the point where Herod is hearing stories about Jesus that trouble him, so that he makes the rather guilty assumption that Jesus might be John the Baptist, returned to life. John the Baptist is already dead at the beginning of this biblical passage, and in the final sentence we are brought full circle to the point at which we started, when John's disciples tell Jesus that John is dead.

While the story tells us quite plainly what a weak man Herod was, it also tells us that he felt guilty or afraid after ordering John's execution. There is also irony in the fact that this story begins with resurrection and ends with death. It is backwards and convoluted. Matthew wants us to know that Herod suspected Jesus to be the reincarnation of John, but he can't tell us that without relating the story of John's demise, which serves to give us a portrait of Herod—his brutality, his weakness, his guilt and his superstitious nature.

The disturbing and poignant tale of the beheading of John the Baptist takes place at Herod's hilltop retreat in present-day Jordan. It is called Machaerus, and all that is left now are a few pillars on top of a commanding position overlooking the Dead Sea, east of the River Jordan. Herod Antipas built there for strategic reasons: he could see the desert fortress of Masada, and smoke signals could be relayed to and from Jerusalem. It was the first line of defence against an attack from the east. Herod also made it an opulent retreat, perhaps not unlike Adolf Hitler's mountain-top 'Eagle's Nest' near Berchtesgaden in Bavaria. Notorious for its tight security, secrecy and expensive price tag, that was an impenetrable bolt-hole with limited access. Anyone can afford to relax in luxury if they are perched atop a mountain in a secure fortress and can see the enemy coming. Hitler and Herod both had the same idea. Ironically, both places are tourist attractions now, memorials to the folly of tyranny and reminders of the depth of evil to which humans can stoop.

The Jewish historian Josephus (AD37–c.100) records that Herod had John the Baptist incarcerated at Machaerus before beheading him. There can be no doubt that John existed, that he annoyed Herod, and that Herod beheaded him accordingly. Matthew's Gospel fleshes out the details, and there is no reason to suppose that the story about Salome dancing and her mother, Herodias, demanding the head of John the Baptist is not true. John was beheaded for upsetting the tyrant whose political methods he was brave enough to criticise. He also challenged Herod's personal sexual ethics, thereby making a double enemy of him. In spite of everything, Herod had been reluctant until that point to do any more to John than lock him up in his hilltop hideaway. Ultimately, John, who only spoke the truth, lost his head for it.

In this much, John was neither the first nor the last. Even today, speaking the truth can lead to persecution, violence and death, even beheading. The American journalist James Foley and the British aid worker David Haines were beheaded by Islamic militants in August and September 2014, as was Daniel Pearl in 2002. Telling the truth can be costly, as much today as ever. The word 'martyr' (which means 'witness', literally) can be used for anyone who has died for a cause or set of beliefs, whether religious or secular. John the Baptist was a martyr, and so is any truth-teller who is murdered for political advantage or publicity, or any aid worker who dies trying to help others.

Not much has changed over the centuries, including our strange relishing of such appalling deeds. Executions by hanging or beheading were, until relatively recently, a public spectacle: the guillotine and gallows once drew large crowds in England and France. People even paid for a better view, and the severed heads were displayed on poles, not only as a warning but for sheer excitement. Various grotesque traditions and superstitions grew up concerning the magical, satanic or even healing properties of such macabre specimens.

Now beheadings have become public once more. Facebook, Twitter and other internet sites have got themselves all tied up over free speech and the dissemination of such material, which, it seems, some folk want to display and others want to see. Some people wring their hands and bemoan how children can and do see such gore (presumably forgetting their visits to the Chamber of Horrors at Madame Tussauds), but it was ever thus, and it is not very long since children were taken to executions for entertainment.

We need to think hard before we flatter ourselves that our world is better or more tolerant, civilised, developed or caring than in the past. We would like it to be so, and, by the grace of God, we have the power to make it so, but it will always be a struggle when there are those who would behave in such barbaric, unjust, selfish and violent ways. When it comes to religious intolerance, political violence, criminal behaviour and freedom of speech, the past is not, as L.P. Hartley once put it, 'a foreign country'; rather, it is somewhere frighteningly familiar.

In modern times of tyranny,
Christ's faithful people always see
that freedom, justice, will prevail
and truth and love shall never fail.

The cost of courage speaking out,
proclaiming truth, without a doubt,
is great and gracious, never cheap
but bold and brave, profoundly deep.

GORDON GILES (b. 1966)

18 December

Going to the synagogue

When [Jesus] came to Nazareth, where he had been brought up, he went to the synagogue on the sabbath day, as was his custom. He stood up to read, and the scroll of the prophet Isaiah was given to him. He unrolled the scroll and found the place where it was written: 'The Spirit of the Lord is upon me, because he has anointed me to bring good news to the poor. He has sent me to proclaim release to the captives and recovery of sight to the blind, to let the oppressed go free, to proclaim the year of the Lord's favour.' And he rolled up the scroll, gave it back to the attendant, and sat down. The eyes of all in the synagogue were fixed on him. Then he began to say to them, 'Today this scripture has been fulfilled in your hearing.' All spoke well of him and were amazed at the gracious words that came from his mouth. They said, 'Is not this Joseph's son?' He said to them, 'Doubtless you will quote to me this proverb, "Doctor, cure yourself!" And you will say, "Do here also in your home town the things that we have heard you did at Capernaum."' And he said, 'Truly I tell you, no prophet is accepted in the prophet's home town...' When they heard this, all in the synagogue were filled with rage. They got up, drove him out of the town, and led him to the brow of the hill on which their town was built, so that they might hurl him off the cliff. But he passed through the midst of them and went on his way.

LUKE 4:16–24, 28–30

We recalled this event when we read about the stoning of Stephen outside Jerusalem (7 December). Just as Stephen was to speak to the Jewish leaders of Jesus' position in the heritage of faith and divine plan for salvation, here Jesus relates himself to that tradition of prophecy, and nearly meets the same fate.

To understand and experience this remarkable event at the beginning of Jesus' public ministry, we might make a journey to the Nazareth Village, open to the public in what is now the largest town with a predominantly Arab population that is actually in the State of Israel rather than in the Palestinian Territories. The reason for this anomaly is that, during the 1948 Arab–Israeli War, the town surrendered to the Israelis on condition that its civilians remained unharmed. The Israeli authorities tried to renege on the deal almost immediately, but the brigade commander who had negotiated the truce with the Palestinians, Ben Dunkelman, stood up for the civilians and refused to allow ethnic cleansing to take place. This makes Nazareth a very unusual place in both Christian and Israeli history and geography. The Nazareth Village, a tourist attraction run by Christians, opened in 2000, having secured a site that had been preserved, through the establishment of the Nazareth Hospital, by the Edinburgh Medical Missionary Society in 1906. Excavations from 1996 onwards have uncovered the site of a wine press that is over 2000 years old, and other historical constructions have been created in the midst of what some might call a theme park, others a fascinating experience of the time of Jesus. As the founder of the Nazareth Village, Dr Nakhle Bishara, put it:

There is a deep desire on the part of all who come to Nazareth to see Jesus. But for centuries, all they could see was dusty stones.

That is why I proposed a place where visitors could see those ancient stones come to life and witness the vineyards and olive trees Jesus used to teach spiritual truth. I am excited that this dream is now a reality. I believe Nazareth Village will be a gift of peace to the world, and also to those of us who live, work, and worship in a land torn by conflict.

WWW.NAZARETHVILLAGE.COM/CATEGORY/65/VISION-AND-PURPOSE

Consequently, visitors today, often in groups, can be shown around the site, on which are a watchtower, olive press, carpenter's workshop, sheepfold, olive trees, farm implements, typical houses and a re-creation of the synagogue in which Jesus' reading from the scroll of Isaiah took place. Visitors may also opt to stay for lunch, when an 'authentic' first-century meal is served. It is an inspiring and informative place and gives a thoroughly engaging experience on any pilgrimage to the Holy Land.

The synagogue on the site is a simple building—rectangular, with an earthen floor and a traditionally made ceiling of straw and clay soil. Held up by pillars, it has a central area where the congregation might stand and a raised area around the inside. When Jesus visited the synagogue in today's story, it was not a special event, and we can picture him reading from the scroll of the prophet Isaiah (Isaiah 61:1–2) in no particularly special way. It was the sabbath, the men were gathered in a normal way, and it was Jesus who was asked to read. Yet we are told that when he had finished, he sat down, perhaps on the stone ledge around the edge of the synagogue. There was tension in the air: clearly the people were expecting some teaching, as they had heard that this son of Nazareth had gained something of a reputation outside the village.

Jesus certainly gives them something to think about. Having read the prophecy, he then says, 'This is me.' The claim impresses them at first, but then he explains how a prophet cannot act in his home town and is rejected by his townsfolk. It is an admission from Jesus that he sees himself at least as a prophet, but, more seriously, as the one to whom the prophecy of Isaiah points—that is, the Messiah. This would have been seen as blasphemy, even in the village synagogue, and that is why the townspeople tried to throw him off a cliff. Doing so conforms with the instruction in the Law to 'stone' blasphemers by throwing them headfirst off a precipice that is at least twice their height (Leviticus 24:13–16).

Jesus escapes to preach another day, returning to Capernaum, where it seems he was much more welcome. From his base there, he begins to call disciples, teach, heal and preach all around the Sea of Galilee, embarking on a ministry that will last more than two years before the Jewish authorities finally lose their patience and can tolerate his good news no more.

He comes the prisoners to release
in Satan's bondage held;
the gates of brass before him burst.
 the iron fetters yield.

He comes the broken heart to bind,
the bleeding soul to cure,
and with the treasures of his grace
to enrich the humble poor.

PHILIP DODDRIDGE (1702–51)

19 December

Going into the wilderness

Then Jesus was led up by the Spirit into the wilderness to be tempted by the devil. He fasted for forty days and forty nights, and afterwards he was famished. The tempter came and said to him, 'If you are the Son of God, command these stones to become loaves of bread.' But he answered, 'It is written, "One does not live by bread alone, but by every word that comes from the mouth of God."' Then the devil took him to the holy city and placed him on the pinnacle of the temple, saying to him, 'If you are the Son of God, throw yourself down; for it is written, "He will command his angels concerning you", and "On their hands they will bear you up, so that you will not dash your foot against a stone."' Jesus said to him, 'Again it is written, "Do not put the Lord your God to the test."' Again, the devil took him to a very high mountain and showed him all the kingdoms of the world and their splendour; and he said to him, 'All these I will give you, if you will fall down and worship me.' Jesus said to him, 'Away with you, Satan! for it is written, "Worship the Lord your God, and serve only him."' Then the devil left him, and suddenly angels came and waited on him.

MATTHEW 4:1–11

In Jericho today you can make a journey on the world's longest below-sea-level cable car. Jericho is on the edge of the Dead Sea, 850 feet below sea level. On the ground, it doesn't look as if it is below sea level; yet, if you start at the bottom of the cable car ride and ascend to 1150 feet above sea level, you get a sense of being much higher up than you actually are. The ascent is to the Mount of Temptation, on top of which is a Greek Orthodox monastery, inhabited by a small group of monks who seldom let visitors in. It is the mountain on which it is supposed that Jesus was tempted by Satan, the mountain from which he was invited to survey and rule all the kingdoms of the world, in return for serving Satan.

The monastery there was built in the sixth century on a site identified by the Emperor Constantine's mother, Helena, in 326. It was through Helena that Constantine became a Christian, and it was under the banner of Christ that he won the battle of Milvian Bridge in October 312. Consequently the Roman Empire became Christian, and the rest, as they say, is history. Helena followed local tradition in saying that the mountain outside Jericho was the place where Jesus had been tempted by Satan, and it is indeed tempting to believe the claim. Whether one can get into the monastery or not, perched on the precipice of a cliff overlooking the Dead Sea and the River Jordan, there are fantastic views to be taken in and a real sense of Holy Land geography to be gained.

The key thing about this place is the view it affords. Mount Tabor, Mount Hermon, Mount Sinai, Mount Nebo—all these high places have spiritual and biblical significance, not only for the events associated with them but for the views they offer. To admire the view is a spiritually uplifting and reflective thing to do.

From the Mount of Temptation, we can see places that resonate with our faith—Jericho, the River Jordan and the Dead Sea. We are physically looking down on the land of

Christ. This in itself is fascinating, but there is also a spiritual viewing. When we consider the temptations of Christ, presented by Matthew and the other Gospel writers near the beginning of their accounts, we are standing at the doorway to Jesus' ministry. Before we read about healings, miracles, teachings and controversies, we meet Jesus being tempted. We read of Jesus, a baby conceived by a virgin and growing through a precocious childhood (of which we have but a glimpse, in Luke's Gospel) into a man with a mission. Yet, before that mission can become a ministry, it is tested by Satan himself.

In the story of Jesus' temptations, we have three classic manifestations of the ways in which Jesus could have failed at the outset: first, the temptation to be dominated by his bodily appetites; second, the temptation to test or control God; and, third, the temptation to sell out and take the easy route. Each of these was a real possibility for Jesus. He could have used his powers and connections to satisfy his own needs and desires; he could have dictated terms to God of how he would go about being the Messiah; or he could have done things the easy way, justifying the end by whatever means. In response to each temptation, Jesus quotes scripture, grounding himself and his future ministry in Jewish tradition, spirituality and obedience. Ultimately, his response to the three temptations is threefold: trust God, obey God, and worship God.

With these three maxims in mind, we can survey the scenes of Jesus' life, ministry, death and resurrection, as well as our own lives. From Jesus' perspective, the view from the top of the mount of temptation is the road to redemption. In the distance we can see Calvary and the shining light of resurrection behind it, opening up the way to glory and eternal life. Before walking the road to Easter, it is good to survey it from a distance, to memorise and mentally map out the landmarks en route. This is why the temptations are often heard in church as we begin Lent. The journey of Lent begins on the Mount of Temptation and ends on the hill of Calvary, with many ups and downs between. In the final few days, Holy Week, we welcome Christ with palm branches and look in horror as the crowd turn against him. We watch him betrayed, arrested, wrongfully tried, flogged and crucified. We walk the way of the cross; we stand and weep at the foot of the cross and then we lay Jesus in Joseph of Arimathea's tomb. Then, with the dawning of Easter Day, we go with Mary and Peter to the tomb and find it empty.

This is the view from atop the Mount of Temptation. It is the view of the journey that the Son of God must take, one step after another—the comings and goings that lead to suffering and death, after which come resurrection hope and light. We know what to look for, and we know what we shall see, because we have looked and walked along this route many times before. We can see into the future liturgically, as it were, because the future looks very like the past. We know how the story goes, and so we can see it coming. We can do this whenever we enter a liturgical season that climaxes with Easter, Christmas or Pentecost. The seasonal rhythms refresh and renew us in remembrance and reflection.

Yet we must not allow ourselves to believe that we know the way, for God always has some surprises. Every Advent is different, because every year *we* are different. Births, deaths, illnesses and other events have changed us since the previous year. Every year we look at our lives through the prism of the Gospels, and we find that we see something different, because we ourselves have been changed, not only by the world, the flesh and the devil but by God in Christ. It is he alone who gives us the power and the will to resist temptation, and the ability to see things as they really are and move forward in our lives in faith, hope and joy.

> Keep, O keep us, Saviour dear,
> Ever constant by Thy side;
> That with Thee we may appear
> At the eternal Eastertide.
>
> GEORGE HUNT SMYTTAN (1822–70)

20 December

Going to a wedding at Cana

On the third day there was a wedding in Cana of Galilee, and the mother of Jesus was there. Jesus and his disciples had also been invited to the wedding. When the wine gave out, the mother of Jesus said to him, 'They have no wine.' And Jesus said to her, 'Woman, what concern is that to you and to me? My hour has not yet come.' His mother said to the servants, 'Do whatever he tells you.' Now standing there were six stone water jars for the Jewish rites of purification, each holding twenty or thirty gallons. Jesus said to them, 'Fill the jars with water.' And they filled them up to the brim. He said to them, 'Now draw some out, and take it to the chief steward.' So they took it. When the steward tasted the water that had become wine, and did not know where it came from (though the servants who had drawn the water knew), the steward called the bridegroom and said to him, 'Everyone serves the good wine first, and then the inferior wine after the guests have become drunk. But you have kept the good wine until now.' Jesus did this, the first of his signs, in Cana of Galilee, and revealed his glory; and his disciples believed in him.

JOHN 2:1–11

There are mysteries of time and place that surround this first of Jesus' signs. First, if we look at the opening chapter of John's Gospel, we see a counting of days, leading up to the placing of this story on the 'third' day (2:1). John begins his Gospel with a theological exposition about the Word becoming flesh (6 January), and then tells us that John testifies to the priests and Levites about his calling as the forerunner of the Messiah. 'The next day' (day two, 1:29), John sees Jesus coming towards him and testifies that he is the Lamb of God. Then, 'the next day' (day three, v. 35), John sees Jesus again, and Jesus calls Andrew and Simon (whom he names 'Cephas'). Another 'next day' follows (day four, v. 43), on which Jesus decides to go to Galilee and calls Nathanael and Philip. Chapter 1 ends with this meeting, and, as we begin chapter 2, John writes, 'On the third day...'. By this he means three days after the calling of Nathanael, which makes it a week after the Gospel begins. In John's description of this first, creative week of Jesus' ministry, there are many comings and goings, which culminate in what the marriage service in the Book of Common Prayer so delightfully calls the 'first miracle that he wrought, in Cana of Galilee'.

Having worked out the timescale, we need to recognise that Cana no longer exists. In fact, there are three places that claim to be the location of Cana, one of which is called Kafr Kanna. Many couples go there today to renew their wedding vows, and there are some wine boutiques that will sell wines of wide-ranging quality to tourists. Putting a label on a bottle of locally produced wine and calling it 'Wine from Cana' gives it a unique selling point, for sure.

The name 'Cana' is derived from Aramaic or Hebrew, meaning 'nest' or 'reeds', a common name for towns. The modern town of Kafr Kanna is only seven miles from Nazareth and an eighth-century tradition identified it as authentic. However, there are other contenders: Ain Kana is closer to Nazareth, while Khirbet Qana claims a tradition of authenticity going back to the Crusader era. Further afield, the historian Eusebius identified Cana as the village of Qana, near Tyre in Lebanon, where it is traditionally revered as the correct site (even though John specifically refers to 'Cana in Galilee'). The fact is that, despite these various claims, each of which has reputable support, we do not know exactly where the biblical Cana was. We do know that the village became embroiled in the rebellion of AD70, which the Romans mercilessly crushed, destroying the Jerusalem temple in the process. Cana served as rebel headquarters in Galilee, so the Romans razed it to the ground. Wherever Cana was, it is no more, and the idea that one can visit the modern village is little more than a lovely idea for romantic couples and wine lovers, even if there are huge stone water jars on display there.

In some sense, Cana is the place where every church wedding takes place. The Christian marriage service refers to Jesus' presence at a wedding in Cana, taking it to be an affirmation of holy matrimony, even though the Gospel narrative is not about marriage *per se*. It is actually about change and new beginnings, which is why such a story sits so well at the beginning of John's Gospel. It also appears frequently in the Epiphany season (the period between Epiphany on 6 January and Candlemas on 2 February). It is allied to the visit of the magi and the baptism of Jesus as one of the three great 'signs' of the light of the world coming to dwell among us as the Word made flesh.

At Cana we meet the freshly baptised Jesus at a wedding feast, which is itself an analogy for the final heavenly banquet to which we are all invited. The Cana wedding feast is a real, commonplace but special event, which marks the beginning and symbolises the meaning of Jesus' ministry on earth. Jesus is going to turn the ordinary into the special, the commonplace into the rare. The involvement of water and wine prefigure his death and resurrection. So the story, like any good wine, can be appreciated on many levels. One is the basic, 'what you see is what you get' level: Jesus goes to a party and helps with the catering. But go a little deeper into those water jars and notice that Jesus is off duty; indeed, he has not, until this point, ever been 'on duty'. John tells us that he did not want to get involved, for being simply a miracle worker (even if that was what Mary wanted) was not part of his plan. Nevertheless, he does accede to Mary's desire and directs the servants to fill the jars. This is how Jesus begins his ministry.

New beginnings are inevitable and cannot be avoided. We are constantly, gradually, affected by the passage of time. People grow up and grow old. We move through education, jobs and retirement. Every now and again we encounter tragedy or pain, in either ourselves or others, and when we do, we find that our living has been both punctured and punctuated. There are many comings and goings in our lives—blips or bumps—and, of course, moments of great joy, with births, marriages and significant birthdays among them. Such are the punctuation marks in the sentence that we might consider to be our lives. Yet Jesus gets involved; he is present by his Spirit and is both an agent of change and the one who is himself changeless.

Manifest at Jordan's stream,
Prophet, Priest, and King supreme;
And, at Cana, wedding-guest
In thy Godhead manifest;
Manifest in power divine,
Changing water into wine;
Anthems be to thee addrest,
God in Man made manifest.

CHRISTOPHER WORDSWORTH (1807–85)

21 December

Jesus goes to John for baptism

John answered them, 'I baptise with water. Among you stands one whom you do not know, the one who is coming after me; I am not worthy to untie the thong of his sandal.' This took place in Bethany across the Jordan where John was baptising. The next day he saw Jesus coming toward him and declared, 'Here is the Lamb of God who takes away the sin of the world! This is he of whom I said, "After me comes a man who ranks ahead of me because he was before me." I myself did not know him; but I came baptising with water for this reason, that he might be revealed to Israel.' And John testified, 'I saw the Spirit descending from heaven like a dove, and it remained on him. I myself did not know him, but the one who sent me to baptise with water said to me, "He on whom you see the Spirit descend and remain is the one who baptises with the Holy Spirit." And I myself have seen and have testified that this is the Son of God.' The next day John again was standing with two of his disciples, and as he watched Jesus walk by, he exclaimed, 'Look, here is the Lamb of God!'
JOHN 1:26–36

Water is a fascinating substance. We are made mostly of it: a few days without it would leave us high and dry (we would lose our minds and soon die). If you know only one chemical formula, it is likely to be H_2O, which means that there is one atom of oxygen bound to two atoms of hydrogen. The hydrogen atoms are 'attached' to one side of the oxygen atom, which causes a water molecule to have a positive charge on the side where the hydrogen atoms are and a negative charge on the other side, where the oxygen atom is. This uneven distribution of charge is known as polarity. As opposite electrical charges attract each other, water molecules tend to attract each other. The molecules stick together, with the hydrogen side of one atom adhering to the oxygen side of the other—a bit like Lego™. This property of water is known as 'cohesion'.

Consequently, all those molecules attracting each other get clumped together into drops of water. There are 1.67×10^{21} molecules in a 0.05 ml drop of water. Water drops are chemically 'sticky', which makes water the universal solvent: other things stick to it too. More substances dissolve into it than into any other liquid, so, wherever water goes, inside or outside our bodies, it transports chemicals, minerals, medicines and nutrients. This property can also be unfortunate, as many nasty diseases are waterborne, causing epidemics.

John the Baptist and Jesus probably weren't thinking about the properties of water when they met on the banks of the River Jordan. It is more likely that they would have been aware of the significance of the Jordan itself, for that river, like any other river, has had a life of its own. Over the years it has moved through the land, taking the path of least resistance as it flows through the Sea of Galilee via Jericho to the Dead Sea. It has ebbed and flowed through biblical times and places.

Nowadays the river does not follow quite the same route as it did 2000 years ago, which means that there are complications concerning the authenticity of the site of Jesus' baptism. Even if we accept the site now known as Bethany by the Jordan, which is accessible from both the Jordanian and the Israeli sides of the river, pilgrims who wish to enter the water are forced to do so a few hundred metres away from the place where the Jordan is thought to have flowed at the time of Jesus. The waters have come and gone for centuries, and the place where the baptism might actually have happened is now dry.

Nevertheless, to visit Bethany by the Jordan can be a profound experience. It is a wonderful place to renew baptismal vows, and in a group it can be inspiring to share stories about one's own baptism. From those who were baptised the day they were born to older Christians who have been baptised by total immersion, the rite of Christian baptism unites us all, even in the diversity of its administration. Sitting on the banks of the Jordan, singing 'On Jordan's bank the Baptist's cry' and seeing white-robed pilgrims being baptised in the waters flowing only a few feet away, one can sense an excitement and spiritual connectedness as new Christians are reborn in the same Spirit that descended on Jesus all those years ago. Christians come and go, but baptismal water bears us all along in a tide of faith that flows into eternal resurrection life. Whether or not the site now visited by thousands in modern Jordan or Israel is precisely accurate geographically, there is a tremendous atmosphere, for here is a location that is not simply a historical site but also a place of living, renewed, modern faith.

It is an evocative place, where we really can connect with the cosmos-altering event in human history, when the man who is God was affirmed by the Holy Spirit descending as a dove. And it all happens in a river made up of that simple, vital substance—water—which carries stuff around the planet in solution, cleansing, feeding and renewing the earth. Water can also be dangerous—swelling, rising and flooding. It presents to us the natural world in its amoral, free, indiscriminate force. We have learned to respect, value, distrust and admire water. To the ancient Greeks, the sea was literally a god, Poseidon, whose anger was felt in the waves.

We would not be here without it. Water is God's gift: earth has 70 per cent of its surface covered in it. Life as we know it is water-based and water-dependent. Our divine Creator used water as the solution for life, so it is no surprise that baptism is done in solution. Water is 'sticky', and so is baptism. The church teaches that a person can be baptised only once. At what age or with what level of commitment is much debated, but Jesus' Jordanian encounter with John connects all Christians to God and each other, not only here and now but also in the past and the future.

Water is the metaphor for our bondedness to God. It reminds us that Christ is God and that we are like Christ. We are bonded to God, and God is the solution for our lives. It is both profound and fitting that water should be the medium, the solution, by which the incarnate Christ is welcomed into a divine ministry of miracles, parables, death, resurrection and salvation. For Christ is the living water, by which we are all cleansed and renewed, bringing us love, mercy and life.

All praise, eternal Son, to thee,
whose advent doth thy people free;
whom with the Father we adore
and Holy Ghost for evermore.
CHARLES COFFIN (1676–1749), TRANS. JOHN CHANDLER (1806–76)

The boy Jesus goes to the temple

Now every year his parents went to Jerusalem for the festival of the Passover. And when he was twelve years old, they went up as usual for the festival. When the festival was ended and they started to return, the boy Jesus stayed behind in Jerusalem, but his parents did not know it. Assuming that he was in the group of travellers, they went a day's journey. Then they started to look for him among their relatives and friends. When they did not find him, they returned to Jerusalem to search for him. After three days they found him in the temple, sitting among the teachers, listening to them and asking them questions. And all who heard him were amazed at his understanding and his answers. When his parents saw him they were astonished; and his mother said to him, 'Child, why have you treated us like this? Look, your father and I have been searching for you in great anxiety.' He said to them, 'Why were you searching for me? Did you not know that I must be in my Father's house?' But they did not understand what he said to them. Then he went down with them and came to Nazareth, and was obedient to them. His mother treasured all these things in her heart. And Jesus increased in wisdom and in years, and in divine and human favour.
LUKE 2:41–52

The Western Wall is all that remains of the temple in Jerusalem. The Romans destroyed the building in AD70, after the Jewish revolt, but they deliberately left the outer wall as an insulting memorial, to remind the population of what had once been and of what could happen if they defied Roman authority and rule. Known as the 'Wailing Wall' to some, it is still a place where Jews congregate to bewail the loss of the temple, and many adopt a posture of lamentation as they lean on the wall. Some insert prayer requests on small scraps of paper into the cracks, while others pray for a day when the temple will be rebuilt (an unlikely possibility, given modern Middle Eastern politics). In Jewish tradition, this is the holiest place on earth, where God is always present. Jewish mystical tradition teaches that all prayers from around the world ascend to the Wall, and from there they ascend heavenwards. To Christians, who have inherited Jesus' proclamation that he is the new temple and that God is present among us by his Spirit, the idea that God has a physical 'home' is alien, but it is real in Judaism and is an ongoing source of regret and hope for restoration.

After the Israeli War of Independence in 1948, the border between Israel and Jordan divided Jerusalem. The Temple Mount, the Jewish Quarter and the Western Wall fell under Jordanian control. Jews were moved out and forbidden to visit the Western Wall. Two decades later, on the third day of the Six-Day War of June 1967, Israel captured the Old City of Jerusalem, including the Western Wall. The buildings close to the wall were removed, and a plaza was built in front of it, enabling thousands to visit the wall daily. At the moment, this is the status quo, and, while there can be tensions that prevent access either to the wall or to the open square above it (where the Islamic Dome of the Rock and Al-Aqsa Mosque are situated), the plaza has become a special place once more, where Jews and others can breathe

the air of faith and history. Many Jewish ceremonies take place there; the site is technically a synagogue, and the wall is partitioned, two-thirds for men and one-third for women. On a Friday evening, as the sabbath begins, the atmosphere can be exciting, even slightly intimidating to visitors, as many Jerusalem Jews like to go to this most holy site as the sun sets. At other times there are invariably Bar Mitzvahs going on, as young Jewish men come of age and take their full place in the worshipping life of Judaism.

The fact that the young Jesus went to the very same place at a similar age makes for a profound juxtaposition of time and place. The context is so different and the time so remote, the geography and skyline so changed, yet the political tensions and physical location are so similar. Jerusalem was a tense place in the first century, and it still is. Occupation, invasion, unrest, religious flare-ups, clamp-downs by the authorities—it still goes on. This is why a visit to the Western Wall and Temple Mount is such a unique experience, for in going there we are transported to a place in our Bibles that we still see on our news bulletins.

We know from this story, unique to Luke's Gospel, that Jesus' parents were in the habit of going to Jerusalem annually. A visit to the temple would have been the highlight. For Jesus, his first visit would have been mesmerising, and he certainly felt at home there, so much so that he did not notice when his parents left. Luke turns the incident into an opportunity to present the paradox of Jesus' being. Having been at pains to tell us that Joseph was not Jesus' biological father and that Mary knew this, he paints her as telling Jesus off for upsetting her and his father, Joseph. The literary twist whereby Jesus and Mary both use the word 'father', but in different senses, reveals the crux of Jesus' sonship. He would go on to teach his disciples to use the Aramaic word *Abba* ('Daddy') for God. He had a personal relationship with his Father in heaven, and would bring that relationship to his followers, too. Meanwhile, Mary sees Joseph as having earthly authority over Jesus, and from this point a gap opens up. Luke tells us that Mary and Joseph simply did not understand what he meant. Nevertheless, he went home with them, submitting to them as parents, observing the commandment to honour his father and mother.

This is a snapshot, a tourist's photo of a moment in Jesus' life that is both ordinary and pivotal. Luke chooses to include it in his Gospel for both reasons: it is an ordinary event, but extraordinary in significance. No one really realised how important it was when it happened, but in quiet recollection Mary remembered. Jesus' words had made little sense at the time, but they took on deep meaning and almost ironical import when he began to teach and preach his way towards Calvary and beyond.

His Father's house he enters in,
Where rabbis teach their cure for sin,
While in his heart he hears the call
Which through his cross won life for all.
GEORGE TIMMS (1910–97)

23 December

Going in haste to Egypt

Now after they had left, an angel of the Lord appeared to Joseph in a dream and said, 'Get up, take the child and his mother, and flee to Egypt, and remain there until I tell you; for Herod is about to search for the child, to destroy him.' Then Joseph got up, took the child and his mother by night, and went to Egypt, and remained there until the death of Herod. This was to fulfil what had been spoken by the Lord through the prophet, 'Out of Egypt I have called my son.' When Herod saw that he had been tricked by the wise men, he was infuriated, and he sent and killed all the children in and around Bethlehem who were two years old or under, according to the time that he had learned from the wise men. Then was fulfilled what had been spoken through the prophet Jeremiah: 'A voice was heard in Ramah, wailing and loud lamentation, Rachel weeping for her children; she refused to be consoled, because they are no more.'

MATTHEW 2:13–18

It is said that on Christmas Day the average Briton consumes 7000 calories and, over the Christmas period, gains about eight pounds in weight. When my daughter was born, she weighed 8lbs 1oz. This means that the average Briton gains the weight of a baby over the Christmas period: during Christmas we can consume and gain the mass of Christ. At this time of year we colloquially refer to 'Christmas cheer', yet, for so many, overeating and drinking too much is not a sign of sheer greed but can disguise mental or emotional torment, lack of self-esteem, grief, loneliness or other troubles. Inevitably there is sadness at Christmas time as well as joy. Christmas can even be the cause of that sadness, especially if the anniversaries of deaths of loved ones or other tragedies occur.

The same is true of the wider world, and Israel, Palestine and Egypt are among the world's greatest trouble spots, just as they were when King Herod ruled as puppet-king of an outpost at the further reaches of the Roman Empire. There is little sign that this will ever change.

Yet into that melée of strife, social injustice, poverty and prejudice was born a baby under rather odd circumstances. The baby Jesus did not appear from nowhere, the result of a bit of end-of-year overindulgence on the part of creative writers called Matthew and Luke. The shepherds in the wilderness outside Bethlehem would, as a group, have been considered reprobates, but they were not sharing a group hallucination when they were summoned to the house where an apparently unremarkable baby had just been brought (or sent) into the world. Nor did the magi trek halfway across the Middle East for nothing. Their visit was sufficiently troubling to King Herod that he had every baby boy slaughtered afterwards. Such calculated horror is hardly fabricated, and is very believable to anyone who knows anything about the megalomaniac, paranoid King Herod. Matthew's Gospel gives us only a snapshot of what Herod was like, but other historians bear out what a nasty piece of work he was. The massacre of the innocents would have been entirely in keeping with his character.

Meanwhile, Joseph is warned to take his family away, reversing the exodus journey, going to rather than coming from Egypt. The facts surrounding this event are disputed; it is not referenced in any other source, but the Egyptian Coptic Church hold it dear in their tradition and have many sites in Egypt that are associated with the journey. In some sources, including those used by Hector Berlioz in his oratorio *L'enfance du Christ* (written in 1854), the family's ultimate destination is considered to be the ancient Egyptian city of Sais. Believed by archaeologists to be in the western Egyptian delta, in modern-day Gharbiyah province, there is still a village called Sa el-Hagar, a name that combines the ancient Egyptian name for the city, 'Sa', with the Arabic word for 'stone'. In the first century this 'stone city' was occupied by the Romans and might have welcomed the itinerant Mary and Joseph, who no doubt had to carry their baby most of the way. If the journey to Bethlehem had its perils and inconveniences, the journey to Egypt would have been much more gruelling.

Even where the facts are easier to glean, we have done a lot to the Christmas story over the years—glammed it up, trivialised it, doubted it, ignored it, hidden it, glossed it over and consumed it. We have consumed the baby Jesus out of the story, covering him in cranberry sauce, brandy cream and millions of tons of chocolate. We have turned his message of salvation and hope into 'Christmas cheer' and drunk it by the festive bottle. If Jesus had had a house and home to be born in, we would have eaten him out of it.

Yet, in a different sense of the word, we should take on board the 'mass' of Christ. The irony of the 8 lb extra weight is clear. Rather than put on 8 lb of Christmas physically, we can try to put Christ on spiritually. Paul wrote, 'For as many of you as were baptised into Christ have put on Christ' (Galatians 3:27, RSV).

If we take the nativity seriously, recognising that God was born among us and became human, dwelling among us, then we can also recognise his call to us to let him be born in us each and every day.

> *O holy Child of Bethlehem, descend to us, we pray;*
> *Cast out our sin, and enter in, be born in us today.*
> *We hear the Christmas angels the great glad tidings tell;*
> *O come to us, abide with us, our Lord Emmanuel!*
> PHILLIPS BROOKS (1835–93)

24 December

Coming to be presented
in the temple

When the time came for their purification according to the law of Moses, they brought him up to Jerusalem to present him to the Lord (as it is written in the law of the Lord, 'Every firstborn male shall be designated as holy to the Lord'), and they offered a sacrifice according to what is stated in the law of the Lord, 'a pair of turtle-doves or two young pigeons'. Now there was a man in Jerusalem whose name was Simeon; this man was righteous and devout, looking forward to the consolation of Israel, and the Holy Spirit rested on him. It had been revealed to him by the Holy Spirit that he would not see death before he had seen the Lord's Messiah. Guided by the Spirit, Simeon came into the temple; and when the parents brought in the child Jesus, to do for him what was customary under the law, Simeon took him in his arms and praised God, saying, 'Master, now you are dismissing your servant in peace, according to your word; for my eyes have seen your salvation, which you have prepared in the presence of all peoples, a light for revelation to the Gentiles and for glory to your people Israel.'...

There was also a prophet, Anna the daughter of Phanuel, of the tribe of Asher. She was of a great age, having lived with her husband for seven years after her marriage, then as a widow to the age of eighty-four. She never left the temple but worshipped there with fasting and prayer night and day. At that moment she came, and began to praise God and to speak about the child to all who were looking for the redemption of Jerusalem.

LUKE 2:22–32, 36–38

It is usually possible for tourists and pilgrims to visit the Temple Mount (Haram al-Sharif) in Jerusalem. Muslims should go up there, Jews must not and Christians may do so, for on a raised area above the former Western Wall of the temple is situated the al-Aqsa Mosque and the Dome of the Rock. The first king of Jordan, Abdullah I, was murdered there and his tomb is nearby. The Dome of the Rock is revered by Muslims as the place from which the prophet Mohammed ascended into heaven, and also by Jews, Christians and Muslims as the place where Isaac was so nearly sacrificed by Abraham (Genesis 22:1–18). Jews may not go there because, since the destruction of the temple by the Romans after the uprising in AD70, no one can be sure where the Holy of Holies was, so it would be possible to transgress its sacred boundaries accidentally. Only priests, such as Zechariah, were allowed to enter that space, and then only once in their lifetime.

For Christians, it is an eerie, yet beautiful place of tranquillity above the hustle and bustle of modern Jerusalem. Despite the security checks, stacked-up riot shields and machine gun-toting guards who nonchalantly stroll around, it is possible to hope for a peaceful visit while being struck by the proximity of violence and danger. When Ariel Sharon visited the site on 28 September 2000 with 1000 policemen and announced that it would always remain under Israeli control, the Palestinians understood him to be laying claim to the site, and a major uprising was ignited. Sharon was elected Israeli Prime Minister within six months.

The temple complex was the holiest site in Judaism, and it was customary for a firstborn male child to be taken there for a ceremony in which he was ritually redeemed (or bought back) from the Lord. The custom derived from the aftermath of the Israelites' flight from Egypt under Moses: in Exodus 13:2 and 11–16, the people are told to dedicate their firstborn sons to God. There was a separate tradition of the purification of the mother, 40 days after a male birth or 80 days after a female birth (Leviticus 12:6–8). It is with this rite of purification that the sacrificial turtle doves are associated: the parents were expected to offer a lamb and a pigeon, or, if they could not afford a lamb, two doves.

Because a mother would not be able to visit the temple within the first 40 days, the two rites were often combined, such that the story in Luke can be a little confusing: Jesus is redeemed and his mother is purified at the same time. We know from the story that Mary and Joseph were devout but poor parents, keen to do the right thing by God and by their rather unusually conceived firstborn son. Nowadays we commemorate this event in the church year as the final day of the 40-day Christmas season—2 February, also known as Candlemas. Simeon was the first to recognise Jesus as the 'light of the Gentiles', the Saviour of all nations, not only the Jews. It was a crucial event, prophetic in its scope as the aged Simeon and Anna recognised and revealed who Jesus was.

There is another, fundamentally human dimension to this story, which any grandparent will recognise. Simeon and Anna were not Jesus' grandparents, of course—they were perhaps more like his godparents—but, as we read of them holding the 40-day-old Christ in their arms, there are resonances for anyone who has held a baby for the first time. There is something wonderfully profound and inherently hopeful as one generation embraces another. In their hopeful embrace of the young Christ, Simeon and Anna show us what it is that we should hope for and embrace. They teach us to relish the salvation we have now seen through their eyes. Whatever age we are, whether we have recently turned 20, 40, 50, 60, 70 or 80, we, like Simeon and Anna, have seen the salvation that has been prepared for us in the birth, death and resurrection of Jesus Christ.

But borne upon the throne
Of Mary's gentle breast,
Watched by her duteous love,
In her fond arms at rest;
Thus to his Father's house
He comes, the heavenly guest.

There Joseph at her side
In reverent wonder stands;
And, filled with holy joy,
Old Simeon in his hands
Takes up the promised Child,
The glory of all lands.

JOHN ELLERTON (1826–93)

25 December

Magi come from the east

In the time of King Herod, after Jesus was born in Bethlehem of Judea, wise men from the East came to Jerusalem, asking, 'Where is the child who has been born king of the Jews? For we observed his star at its rising, and have come to pay him homage.' When King Herod heard this, he was frightened, and all Jerusalem with him; and calling together all the chief priests and scribes of the people, he inquired of them where the Messiah was to be born. They told him, 'In Bethlehem of Judea; for so it has been written by the prophet: "And you, Bethlehem, in the land of Judah, are by no means least among the rulers of Judah; for from you shall come a ruler who is to shepherd my people Israel."'

Then Herod secretly called for the wise men and learned from them the exact time when the star had appeared. Then he sent them to Bethlehem, saying, 'Go and search diligently for the child; and when you have found him, bring me word so that I may also go and pay him homage.' When they had heard the king, they set out; and there, ahead of them, went the star that they had seen at its rising, until it stopped over the place where the child was. When they saw that the star had stopped, they were overwhelmed with joy. On entering the house, they saw the child with Mary his mother; and they knelt down and paid him homage. Then, opening their treasure-chests, they offered him gifts of gold, frankincense, and myrrh. And having been warned in a dream not to return to Herod, they left for their own country by another road.

MATTHEW 2:1–12

It is unusual to hear this text read in church on Christmas Day, as it is usually reserved for the celebration of the Epiphany on 6 January. It is generally reckoned that the wise men, or magi (but not 'kings'!), visited Jesus some long while, even years, after he was born, but the shepherds arrived much sooner. Only at carol services do we hear the two accounts in quick succession, reinforcing a skewed timescale of events. The classic crib scene involves shepherds and magi simultaneously kneeling at the manger, which is depicted as a feeding trough, full of hay, raised on legs. Ox and ass attend, and sometimes other animals. At St Paul's Cathedral in London they have a life-sized wooden crib scene, which includes a wonderful carving of a former Dean's dog.

The origins of this tradition can be found in Francis of Assisi's 'invention' of the crib scene in Greccio in 1223. Exactly as he intended, it captured the imagination of the townspeople and slid into the Christmas culture of the Christian world. Even today, crib services, often aimed at young children, are some of the best-attended church services of the year. In my own parish we have to do ours twice on Christmas Eve afternoon because it is so popular. Like so many parish churches, we stage a 'live' crib scene, with verses from Christmas carols punctuating a semi-dramatic, costumed presentation of the nativity. The angel Gabriel wears white, the shepherds are rustically dressed, and the magi are resplendent in fine robes, walking down the aisle with their three gifts, accompanied by a rendition of 'We three kings'. While Matthew does not say that there

were three of them or that they were kings, John Henry
Hopkins' carol of 1857 does tell us what the gifts mean:

Born a king on Bethlehem's plain,
Gold I bring to crown him again,
King for ever, ceasing never,
Over us all to reign.

Frankincense to offer have I;
Incense owns a deity nigh;
Prayer and praising, voices raising,
Worshipping God on high.

Myrrh is mine, its bitter perfume
Breathes a life of gathering gloom;
Sorrowing, sighing, bleeding, dying,
Sealed in the stone-cold tomb.

JOHN HENRY HOPKINS JR (1820–91)

Here is prophecy contained within the Gospel: the three gifts
have meanings that connect the presence of Christ to the
present offered. The 'mystic meaning' of the gifts points us
forwards to Christ's death and beyond. In a sense they are in
the wrong order, for, temporally speaking, the list should read
'myrrh, gold and frankincense'. Here at the birth of Jesus, his
death and resurrection are prefigured in the gift of myrrh,
an embalming spice. The prophetic gift is realised in John
19:39: 'Nicodemus, who had at first come to Jesus by night,
also came, bringing a mixture of myrrh and aloes, weighing
about a hundred pounds.' The gift of gold indicates kingship,
which is fully realised in Jesus after the ascension: 'But of
the Son he says, "Your throne, O God, is for ever and ever,
and the righteous sceptre is the sceptre of your kingdom"'

(Hebrews 1:8). There are many overtones of Christ's kingship in the Gospels, such as his transfiguration (16 December) and the triumphal entry into Jerusalem associated with Palm Sunday, but it is after his ascension that we tend to see Christ as seated in glory, reigning with the Father and the Spirit in trinitarian unity. In that context and rôle, we worship Christ as king and Saviour, which makes the incense, still used in many churches to assist prayer and praise, the third gift to become relevant. Frankincense is a present that betokens the presence of God, who is to be worshipped and adored: 'Let my prayer be counted as incense before you, and the lifting up of my hands as an evening sacrifice' (Psalm 141:2).

This attempt to reorder the gifts reveals a fundamental flaw, which is that all three of them represent something 'outside' time as we know it. When we read of the magis' presents, we know the events and contexts that they prefigure; and when we read of wise Nicodemus providing myrrh for burial, we remember that he first came to Jesus by night (John 3:2) and that the magi brought myrrh for Jesus. This connects Nicodemus with the magi, and it connects Jesus' birth with his resurrection.

This connectability is the key to Christmas, for it brings together Christ's coming and his going. There is but a short span, less than what we would consider a lifetime, between these two earth-shattering and time-bending events. The earthly, temporal life of Christ was minute cosmologically but hugely significant soteriologically (that is, in terms of our salvation). That such a small piece of time could manifest something so enormous as incarnation is the greater miracle reflected in the face of a small, helpless infant who was to become the most significant human being on earth or in heaven—Jesus Christ, the prince of peace and king of glory.

By its lambent beauty guided,
See, the Eastern kings appear;
See them bend, their gifts to offer,
Gifts of incense, gold, and myrrh.

Offerings of mystic meaning!
Incense doth the God disclose;
Gold a royal child proclaimeth;
Myrrh a future tomb foreshows.
AURELIUS CLEMENS PRUDENTIUS (348–405)

26 December

Shepherds come from the fields

In that region there were shepherds living in the fields, keeping watch over their flock by night. Then an angel of the Lord stood before them, and the glory of the Lord shone around them, and they were terrified. But the angel said to them, 'Do not be afraid; for see—I am bringing you good news of great joy for all the people: to you is born this day in the city of David a Saviour, who is the Messiah, the Lord. This will be a sign for you: you will find a child wrapped in bands of cloth and lying in a manger.' And suddenly there was with the angel a multitude of the heavenly host, praising God and saying, 'Glory to God in the highest heaven, and on earth peace among those whom he favours!'

When the angels had left them and gone into heaven, the shepherds said to one another, 'Let us go now to Bethlehem and see this thing that has taken place, which the Lord has made known to us.' So they went with haste and found Mary and Joseph, and the child lying in the manger. When they saw this, they made known what had been told them about this child; and all who heard it were amazed at what the shepherds told them. But Mary treasured all these words and pondered them in her heart. The shepherds returned, glorifying and praising God for all they had heard and seen, as it had been told them.

LUKE 2:8–20

The little town of Bethlehem is currently in the Palestinian Territories of the central West Bank. Just over four miles from Jerusalem, it is a tourist and pilgrim draw, mostly for the Church of the Nativity and the outlying Shepherds' Fields site. The town also has a piece of graffiti art by the world-famous Banksy, depicting a dove with an olive branch in its beak, and with the cross-hairs of a sniper's rifle visible on the breast of its flak jacket. It is Banksy's statement about peace in the place where the Prince of Peace was brought into the world, and it resonates with the dove sent out from Noah's ark, which returned with an olive leaf as a sign of hope for a new beginning (Genesis 8:11). The idea of Bethlehem as a place where we might hope for new beginnings is poignant when we recall that it is Jesus' birthplace and a location where so much Israeli–Palestinian strife has occurred, most notably in 2002, when there was a 39-day siege of the town.

Bethlehem means 'house of bread' in Aramaic and Hebrew and 'house of meat' in Arabic. It is an ancient town, first mentioned in the Bible as the burial place of Jacob's wife Rachel (Genesis 35:19; 48:7). One of Israel's judges, Ibzan, was from Bethlehem (Judges 12:8). More famously, Elimelech and Naomi originated from Bethlehem but moved to Moab because of famine (Ruth 1:1–2). After her husband and sons died, Naomi returned to Bethlehem with her Moabite daughter-in-law Ruth (v. 22). Ruth married Boaz the Bethlehemite (4:13) and their son, Obed, became the father of Jesse, who was the father of David (v. 17). Thus the idea of Bethlehem as David's town was established, and Jesus' birth there gives the town a past and future significance. In Advent carol services we often look forward to the birth of Jesus by looking back at the prophecy in Micah that says, 'But you, O Bethlehem of Ephrathah, who are one of the little clans of Judah, from you shall come forth for me one who is to rule in Israel, whose origin is from of old, from ancient days' (Micah 5:2).

During Advent we generally look forward by looking back, anticipating the birth of Jesus at Bethlehem by reminding ourselves of the Old Testament prophecies that weave a predictive journey from the most ancient of days. So, then, in church we have journeyed to the Christmas manger by following a path of prophecy from the past, but in this book we have been tracing a path of life, death and resurrection stretching backwards from the future. Here, on Boxing Day, we have arrived at the meeting point, where past, present and future coincide—a crossroads of birth and death, where meanings compound as events collide. The Old Testament looks forward to this place and point in time when the Messiah will be born, and the New Testament looks backward to it and emerges from it. Tomorrow, when we enter the Church of the Nativity, we shall be standing at that turning point in world history, to which all the past and all the future looks, from before and after.

Birth and death intertwine at Bethlehem, and, just as the cross points us back to the birth, the birth points us forward to the cross. The wood of the cradle and the beam of the cross are one and the same. There is ironic significance in the fact that Joseph was a worker in wood and stone (as we shall see on 29 December). Old and new covenants meet here in Bethlehem, the place where it all ends and begins.

At this meeting point of time and place, we find shepherds and angels coming and going. They represent the earthly and the heavenly. Just as past and future coincide and collide here, so do earth and heaven, and their inhabitants face one another at this unique juncture. Overlooked, smelly, disreputable sheep-minders are disturbed and distressed by angels giving the first rendition of the 'Gloria in excelsis'. The shepherds are given an insight into the ways of God and sent to greet the weakling infant in whose tiny hands the world's future is held. They set off, under ethereal instruction, knowing full well that no one will believe them when they relate their bizarre nocturnal escapade. Yet they become the world's most acclaimed shepherds, famous in the future to billions, many of whom draw inspiration from their humility, obedience and devotion.

Today, the place where the world believes they had their experience is a beautiful place of pilgrimage, where groups can celebrate Holy Communion and sing 'While shepherds watched' in the open air or in a grotto. Pilgrims are reminded of the shepherds while overlooking a modern Jewish settlement built in Palestinian territories and bounded by razor wire, betokening a fragile peace.

Why lies he in such mean estate,
Where ox and ass are feeding?
Good Christians, fear; for sinners here
The silent Word is pleading.
Nails, spear shall pierce Him through,
The cross be borne for me, for you.
Hail, hail the Word made flesh,
The Babe, the Son of Mary.

WILLIAM CHATTERTON DIX (1837–98)

27 December

Christmas comes to the Church of the Nativity

In those days a decree went out from Emperor Augustus that all the world should be registered. This was the first registration and was taken while Quirinius was governor of Syria. All went to their own towns to be registered. Joseph also went from the town of Nazareth in Galilee to Judea, to the city of David called Bethlehem, because he was descended from the house and family of David. He went to be registered with Mary, to whom he was engaged and who was expecting a child. While they were there, the time came for her to deliver her child. And she gave birth to her firstborn son and wrapped him in bands of cloth, and laid him in a manger, because there was no place for them in the inn.

LUKE 2:1–7

The Church of the Nativity in Bethlehem takes on a special feel as pilgrims flock there to celebrate Jesus' birth in the place where it most probably happened. Many feel warm and cosy about the idea of being 'there', celebrating and worshipping in a church built over a site where it is supposed that the incarnation actually occurred. Notwithstanding the potentially huge queues (sometimes up to three hours long), pilgrims can descend to an underground cave, lit with candles, where there is a hole in the ground with a star around it. There, they can kneel and place a hand on the spot, identified centuries ago and revered ever since, where Mary gave birth—the place where the Messiah was born, where God took our human flesh and came to dwell among us, and where Helena is supposed to have discovered the actual manger (now in the Basilica of Santa Maria Maggiore, in Rome). The church is undoubtedly a very holy place, and its doorway is deliberately half-sized so that one must stoop to enter, to adopt the form and stature of a child, whose simple faith Jesus himself praised (Mark 10:15).

If we are trying to 'locate' the incarnation—the blending of humanity and divinity that we find in Jesus—then the Church of the Nativity makes the greatest claim. Even if we doubt that the 'manger' on display is authentic, and if we consider the star-shaped touching spot to be a gimmick, there is a real sense that this dark, humid cave is a place where many have knelt before, where prayers and devotions have been offered and succour felt. Just as we can do in the Church of the Holy Sepulchre, where there is a similar star-shaped opening in the ground (see 13 December), we exchange doubts and details for devotion, offering prayer and thanksgiving in a living space of faith where countless others have done the same. It may or may not be the literal place of incarnation, but it is a bounded space where attention has been focused like a laser on to the very hub of faith: 'For God so loved the world that he gave his only Son, so that everyone who believes in him may not perish but may have eternal life. Indeed, God did not send the Son into the world to condemn the world, but in order that the world might be saved through him' (John 3:16–17).

Pilgrims to the Holy Land these days often visit Jerusalem before Bethlehem, which means that they will kneel at the two stars in the ground, at the Church of the Nativity and the

Holy Sepulchre, in the 'wrong' order (and one does have to kneel down in both places). A pilgrim in Bethlehem is very likely to be staying in Jerusalem, and so may well have visited the Holy Sepulchre on the first day, perhaps walking the Via Dolorosa. As in this book, the events are topsy-turvy, which makes them look, and feel, rather odd. Kneeling at the star of Bethlehem recalls the star of Calvary, and reminds us, as so many Christmas carols do, of the babe of Bethlehem who was born to die for our salvation. We visit the manger having seen the cross, so we know what is coming. The fact that the experiences in both places are identical—we are on our knees with our hand placed on a piece of rock—makes the connection between divine birth and suffering inexorable. It doesn't matter whether the locations are precisely accurate or, indeed, even completely spurious. What is important is that we are in a place where people have prayed for centuries and where the Holy Spirit makes connections in us that carry us through life. Furthermore, the sense of a holy place, in which this happens, adds a unique and memorable profundity and purpose.

Many people sing at the place of Jesus' birth. I have heard 'Away in a manger' sung to the tunes used in the UK ('Cradle song', written by William Kirkpatrick in 1895) and the USA ('Mueller' by James Murray, written in 1887). The two tunes, being straightforward and in the same key, actually work as counterparts to each other: the tunes can be sung simultaneously. Some groups sing 'O little town of Bethlehem'. These holy walls have absorbed not only prayers but also songs. The familiar, somewhat romanticised carols resonate with our celebrations of Christmas at the 'Nine lessons and carols' or a simple candle-lit carol service. By bringing our carols into this holy place, we are singing where others have sung, bringing something of our homely worship to Bethlehem, and taking something of Bethlehem home with us.

But what are we taking home? Bethlehem is not a place of peace where the little Lord Jesus makes no crying, nor is it a place of silence where the wondrous gift of God is given. It is, sadly, a focal point for the ongoing Palestinian–Israeli conflicts, and sometimes it has not been safe to visit. Some Christmases past have been marred by gunfire, with the lowly half-sized door closed to pilgrims.

As my friend, the hymn writer Martin Leckebusch, once put it in a variant of 'O little town':

O West Bank town of Bethlehem,
how still thy victims lie;
the grieving weep, deprived of sleep;
militia men roam by;
for through thy dark streets rageth
the never-ending fight:
such hopes and fears, such bitter tears
are met in thee tonight.

MARTIN LECKEBUSCH (b. 1963)

Rather as we can sing 'Away in a manger' to two tunes or have two sets of words for a familiar tune, we need to weave Christmas past with Christmas present. We may celebrate the joy to the world that God's gift of Jesus is to us; but we must also lament the reality that the gift of peace and goodwill from on high, proclaimed by the angels, is yet to be unwrapped in the very place where it was first delivered.

Yet with the woes of sin and strife
The world has suffered long;
Beneath the angel strain have rolled
Two thousand years of wrong;
And man, at war with man, hears not
The love-song which they bring;
O hush the noise, ye men of strife,
And hear the angels sing.

EDMUND HAMILTON SEARS (1810–76)

28 December

Going to work with Joseph

When his mother Mary had been engaged to Joseph, but before they lived together, she was found to be with child from the Holy Spirit. Her husband Joseph, being a righteous man and unwilling to expose her to public disgrace, planned to dismiss her quietly. But just when he had resolved to do this, an angel of the Lord appeared to him in a dream and said, 'Joseph, son of David, do not be afraid to take Mary as your wife, for the child conceived in her is from the Holy Spirit. She will bear a son, and you are to name him Jesus, for he will save his people from their sins.' All this took place to fulfil what had been spoken by the Lord through the prophet: 'Look, the virgin shall conceive and bear a son, and they shall name him Emmanuel', which means, 'God is with us.' When Joseph awoke from sleep, he did as the angel of the Lord commanded him; he took her as his wife, but had no marital relations with her until she had borne a son; and he named him Jesus.

MATTHEW 1:18–25

In Matthew's Gospel, this account immediately precedes the account of the visit of the magi. There are no shepherds mentioned; the magi are the only visitors, arriving some time between the birth of Jesus and the family's flight into Egypt, the prompt for which is another dream (Matthew 2:13–15). Then we hear of Herod killing the little boys under the age of two (v. 16). However, in our carol services and Christmas sequences of readings, we interweave the accounts of Luke and Matthew, which, although the two Gospels are by no means incompatible, does sometimes obscure the thread and thrust of each separate account.

Luke is interested in Mary, the shepherds and the angels. Matthew is interested in Joseph, dreams and the magi. Neither of them tells us much about Joseph, and he disappears— missing, presumed dead—after the occasion when Jesus gets left behind in the temple (Luke 2:41–51)). But who was Joseph? What do we know about him? It is clear that he was a righteous man, someone who followed the law and, although he could have made a disgrace of Mary, chose not to. Matthew tells us much later (13:55) that Joseph was a 'carpenter' (*tekton*), or, rather, that Jesus was described by those in the synagogue as 'the carpenter's son'. This is telling because it reveals that whatever rumours may have been around at the time of Jesus' birth, they had been absorbed, overlooked or forgotten. Jesus was considered to be Joseph's son, and Joseph was a carpenter.

However, this traditional English translation of the Greek word *tekton* is too simple, even inaccurate. Our words 'technology' and 'technique' derive from the same root, and, in Plato's Greek, *techné* is the idea from which we have evolved the notions of both art and craft (a distinction not recognised in classical Greek). The suffix of the word 'archi-tect' is derived from *tekton*, and in this case it means 'builder', not carpenter. So Joseph was not simply a carpenter, working only with wood (of which there wasn't much to be found), but also a stonemason—a builder of houses rather than a maker of furniture. This was the trade into which Jesus was initiated as a boy.

Less than an hour's walk from Nazareth, where Joseph and his family settled after returning from Egypt, is the wonderful Roman town of Sepphoris. Its ruins are still accessible and are worth visiting in their own right. Sepphoris was the provincial capital of Galilee, and around AD3 it was a hive of activity, a major centre of employment for *tektons* like Joseph, because it was being rebuilt. It may be that Joseph decided to settle in Galilee precisely because there would be plenty of work nearby. Some traditions also locate the home of Joachim and Anna, Mary's parents, in Sepphoris. Around 4BC, after the death of Herod the Great, Sepphoris was ransacked by rebels led by Judas, son of Ezekias, so Herod's successor, Herod Antipas, decided to rebuild it as the 'ornament' of the Galilee region. It had streets laid out in a grid pattern, with limestone pavements, and elegant houses and public buildings, as well as a large amphitheatre. Beautiful mosaics can still be seen there, and one can walk among the ruins with an awareness that Jesus may have walked the very same streets as a young man.

A town loyal to Rome and influenced by Greek culture, there is a strong possibility that Sepphoris was well known by Jesus, and he may have worked there with his father as a *tekton*. His frequent use of the word 'hypocrite' (literally 'play actor') when criticising others indicates a knowledge of the theatre, which may have been gleaned from seeing plays in the amphitheatre there. Similarly, Jesus used house-building analogies—for example, when he said that the foundations of a house should be built on rock rather than sand (Luke 6:48–49).

If there is any mileage in the claim that Joseph worked at Sepphoris, then we may say that he took very seriously his responsibility to his rather unusually conceived family.

A righteous, hardworking, skilled artisan, he adopted, protected, trained and loved Jesus, perhaps little knowing where it would all lead. He was an agent of God's will, whose actions prepared Jesus for adulthood. We have already seen how Joseph took Mary and the baby Jesus to the temple after 40 days (see 24 December), and how Simeon and Anna may have given him an inkling of what Jesus' destiny might be. While we are told that Mary 'pondered' and preserved memories in her heart, we have no idea what Joseph thought. Yet he was a reflective man, whose faith, obedience, integrity and service are an inspiration to any man or woman.

As Joseph was a-walking,
he heard an angel sing:
'This night there shall be born
on earth our heavenly king.'
ENGLISH TRADITIONAL CAROL

29 December

The angel Gabriel comes to Mary

In the sixth month the angel Gabriel was sent by God to a town in Galilee called Nazareth, to a virgin engaged to a man whose name was Joseph, of the house of David. The virgin's name was Mary. And he came to her and said, 'Greetings, favoured one! The Lord is with you.' But she was much perplexed by his words and pondered what sort of greeting this might be. The angel said to her, 'Do not be afraid, Mary, for you have found favour with God. And now, you will conceive in your womb and bear a son, and you will name him Jesus. He will be great, and will be called the Son of the Most High, and the Lord God will give to him the throne of his ancestor David. He will reign over the house of Jacob for ever, and of his kingdom there will be no end.' Mary said to the angel, 'How can this be, since I am a virgin?' The angel said to her, 'The Holy Spirit will come upon you, and the power of the Most High will overshadow you; therefore the child to be born will be holy; he will be called Son of God. And now, your relative Elizabeth in her old age has also conceived a son; and this is the sixth month for her who was said to be barren. For nothing will be impossible with God.' Then Mary said, 'Here am I, the servant of the Lord; let it be with me according to your word.' Then the angel departed from her.

LUKE 1:26–38

This passage will have been read many times at carol services over the past weeks, in many languages and in many places, from schools to old people's homes, in medieval churches and baroque cathedrals, at beach services in the southern hemisphere and on wet and windy Sunday evenings in the northern hemisphere. Some such events will have been the 'Service of Nine Lessons and Carols', others informal worship. A church near me in north London even conducts baptisms at its crib service on Christmas Eve, in an unusual, unexpected and rather lovely juxtaposition of birth, hope and commitment.

Birth, hope and commitment are, in fact, what today's Bible passage is all about. In this 'present' moment, when Mary is surprised by a heavenly messenger, everything he says both emerges from the past and is future-orientated. There are different futures involved, though—immediate, quite soon, a little later, distant and on to eternity. All are packed into this revelatory moment, out of which unfolds absolutely everything else.

First, there is that instant for Mary when the very notion of the present moment is rocked. She must have been a little dazed, wondering whether this strange occurrence was actually happening or whether it was a dream or an illusion: 'Who is this stranger coming to see me?' Having wondered what on earth is going on, she soon composes herself and hears news of something that will happen immediately. Before the angel came, she was presumably not pregnant. He tells her that soon the Holy Spirit will make her so. This is an immediate prediction of something that is very imminent indeed.

This bombshell is immediately followed by another, even more pressing revelation. Mary's relative, Elizabeth, has already begun her own improbable journey of pregnancy and will give birth in three months' time. It seems that Mary does not already know this, but the birth of the boy who will be called John will happen quite soon. One of Mary's first actions after the annunciation is to go and visit the older woman.

A slightly later future will become reality as Mary grows with child, to face a gruelling journey to Bethlehem and the ignominy of giving birth in a crude animal house. Far more importantly, she is being told that her child (of whose conception she has heard only seconds earlier) will be the Son of God, heir to the throne of David and king of Israel. The angel is telling Mary that the future hope of the past is about to become real and actual, and it will be her job literally to deliver it to the world. Biological and social restrictions notwithstanding, this is the future that will come even later—childbirth with all its theological and historical trimmings.

After birth comes motherhood, another huge responsibility, with which an unexpectedly pregnant mother must come to terms in advance. It may not have dawned on her immediately, but single motherhood would not be easy, physically, emotionally, socially or culturally. Racing through her mind might have been the niggling question, 'What is Joseph going to say and do?' So while the angel Gabriel is telling her about the fulfilment of past prophecy, she is projecting her mind forward to the changed, unknown life of love and care that will surely follow.

Finally, there is the eternal dimension. Gabriel has used phrases like 'for ever' and 'without end' in describing the kingdom that this as-yet-unconceived divine and human being will inherit. In this birth-to-be, the hopes (and fears) of all the years are met together in one small package that will change the direction of the world, like a theological 'Big Bang'.

All that is needed is commitment—Mary's commitment.

The account we have of the encounter between Gabriel and Mary is stylised, and we might need to do some reading between the lines. On the surface, Gabriel tells her that she will have a divine child, and having been informed that Elizabeth is in a similarly surprising situation, Mary simply says what amounts to 'OK, then.' After all, Elizabeth is so ancient and decrepit that her pregnancy must be a miracle, a bit like Sarah's in Genesis 18:1–15. Unlike Sarah, though, Mary does not laugh; she accepts the will and call of God. This makes her not weak but strong, and it betokens a depth and quality of commitment that is almost unknown to modern society. Most people nowadays will abandon anything to which they have committed themselves, given the right (or wrong) circumstances. Whether in relationships, parenthood, military action or business life, loyalty and commitment are not as they used to be understood.

This is why Mary's commitment is so revered in every time and place. In Nazareth today there is a modern Basilica of the Annunciation, built by Giovanni Muzio in 1969. It replaced an 18th-century church, which had itself surmounted the ruins of both a Crusader-era and, before that, a Byzantine church marking the place where the annunciation is supposed to have occurred. (The Orthodox tradition reveres a well in Nazareth instead, and this too is now a holy site.) Inside the basilica are many mosaics and depictions of the annunciation from different countries and Christian traditions. Some are artistically better than others, but it is remarkable to see how wide is the influence and inspiration of this singular event in history. Imagery from all corners of the globe adorn the church, all depicting the same story of how a young first-century Palestinian girl became the *theotokos* ('bearer of God') to the world. From her commitment to that task springs our hope and our salvation.

> *Blest in the message Gabriel brought;*
> *Blest in the work the Spirit wrought;*
> *Most blest, to bring to human birth*
> *The long-desired of all the earth.*

VENANTIUS HONORIUS CLEMANTIANUS FORTUNATUS (C.535–609),
TRANS. JOHN MASON NEALE (1818–66)

30 December

The promised land comes into view

On that very day the Lord addressed Moses as follows: 'Ascend this mountain of the Abarim, Mount Nebo, which is in the land of Moab, across from Jericho, and view the land of Canaan, which I am giving to the Israelites for a possession; you shall die there on the mountain that you ascend and shall be gathered to your kin, as your brother Aaron died on Mount Hor and was gathered to his kin; because both of you broke faith with me among the Israelites at the waters of Meribath-kadesh in the wilderness of Zin, by failing to maintain my holiness among the Israelites. Although you may view the land from a distance, you shall not enter it—the land that I am giving to the Israelites.'

DEUTERONOMY 32:48–52

This brief passage describing Moses' final encounter with the Lord is one of the most significant in the Bible. As we approach the end of our Advent and Christmas journey, we now go to the top of Mount Nebo at a moment in history, the repercussions of which are still unfolding in the Middle East today. So much of the trouble we see in that region is, at root, all about land, and can be traced back to ancient biblical understandings of nationhood. In this passage, Moses meets God on a mountain (not for the first time) and is shown the 'promised land' of Canaan—the Israelites' goal at the end of 40 years of wandering in the wilderness after their flight from the Egyptians. Lying between the River Jordan and the Mediterranean Sea, it is the land first promised to Abraham, Isaac and Jacob (Genesis 15:18–21; 28:13).

The names of the countries that fall within its compass have changed over the centuries. Tribes have come and gone; cities have risen and fallen, yet there is a connectedness to the land for modern Israelis and Palestinians alike, whose conflicts since the creation of the modern State of Israel in 1948 show little sign of abatement or resolution any time soon. While modern Palestinians speak Arabic and are often contrasted culturally with Israeli Jews, recent research suggests that 70 per cent of modern Israeli Jews and 82 per cent of modern Palestinian Muslims share a genetic (Y chromosome) pool that relates them inexorably. Furthermore, this genetic link can be traced back within the western lands of the Middle East (the 'Levant') to a mix of Muslims, Jews and Christians. Jewish Palestinians rarely identify themselves as such nowadays, whereas Christian Palestinians constitute six per cent of all Palestinians, but at least half have moved away from the region. Ninety-three per cent of Palestinians are Muslims, probably descended from those who converted to Islam in the seventh century. Consequently it should be acknowledged that while Palestinian Jews, Christians and Muslims are members of different faith communities nowadays, their genetic and cultural origins are fundamentally the same. This makes the conflicts in the Middle East all the more tragic.

When Moses stood on top of Mount Nebo and looked towards what is now Jerusalem, he could not have foreseen any of this. Yet, despite the passage of time, the view cannot have changed very much. One can still go to the top of Mount Nebo (now in Jordan) and look across a fantastic desert landscape that will have remained much the same since Moses' day. On one occasion, while admiring the view up there, I met someone who said that when his father was a boy he used to walk to Jerusalem (a distance of 46 km). On a very fine day, Jerusalem is visible, and the city of Jericho (27 km away) can also be seen. Although there is still scholarly debate over whether the current Mount Nebo is the mountain referred to in the book of Deuteronomy, it is associated with Moses' place of death and burial, at least in the Christian tradition. In 1933, archaeologists discovered a fourth-century monastery on the summit, mentioned by the pilgrim Egeria in 397 and rebuilt in 597. Now there is also a striking sculpture by the Italian Giovanni Fantoni, depicting a bronze serpent and the cross intertwined. The sculptor thus reminds us not only of the story of Moses holding up the serpent for healing in the wilderness (Numbers 21:4–9) but also of the direct comparison made between Jesus and Moses in John's Gospel: 'Just as Moses lifted up the serpent in the wilderness, so must the Son of Man be lifted up, that whoever believes in him may have eternal life' (John 3:14–15).

When one stands on top of Mount Nebo, the Old and New Testaments collide in a powerful and profound scene of visual beauty and political history. Jesus stands in the tradition of Moses, and we are reminded of the occasion when he was transfigured, appearing with Moses and Elijah on top of what might have been Mount Tabor (16 December). Nowadays the connection is also made on Nebo, where Moses said farewell and saw the promised land. In the bronze serpent entwined with the cross are two symbols connecting the heroes of Old and New Testaments—Moses, who led the Israelites out of Egypt to freedom, and Jesus, who, as Messiah, leads God's people to a new freedom opened up in redemption and love.

We are returning towards the beginning of all things, and here we pause and take stock, overlooking centuries of spiritual and political history, which finds its roots in Moses and Abraham. We have arrived at a high point, but it is also a point at which the three great faiths of Judaism, Christianity and Islam converge. Moses ('Musa' to Muslims) is a father in faith to us all. Yet nations and peoples have continually fought over this land and about their faith, and have competed for resources, especially water and pasture, where they have been scarce. Our prayer and hope must be that the nations of the world might live together in peace and mutual understanding and tolerance, while humbly affirming the distinctive nature of their heritages, cultures and faiths.

In Jesus Christ we see the culmination of ancient faith and human history, and we have a model for divine and human love that has the power to transcend our divisions. As Christians, surveying the span of history and space from the perspective of the cross and resurrection, we can truly live and share the good news of healing, reconciliation and love, offered by God in Christ to each and every person in every age and place.

O Lord, once lifted on the glorious tree,
As thou has promised, draw us unto thee:
Lift high the cross, the love of Christ proclaim
Till all the world adore his sacred name.
GEORGE WILLIAM KITCHEN (1827–1912)

31 December

Moses goes to get the ten commandments

Then God spoke all these words: I am the Lord your God, who brought you out of the land of Egypt, out of the house of slavery; you shall have no other gods before me. You shall not make for yourself an idol, whether in the form of anything that is in heaven above, or that is on the earth beneath, or that is in the water under the earth... You shall not make wrongful use of the name of the Lord your God, for the Lord will not acquit anyone who misuses his name. Remember the sabbath day, and keep it holy. For six days you shall labour and do all your work... Honour your father and your mother, so that your days may be long in the land that the Lord your God is giving you. You shall not murder. You shall not commit adultery. You shall not steal. You shall not bear false witness against your neighbour. You shall not covet your neighbour's house; you shall not covet your neighbour's wife, or male or female slave, or ox, or donkey, or anything that belongs to your neighbour.

EXODUS 20:1–4, 7–9, 12–17

The ten commandments lie at the foundations of Christianity, Judaism and Islam. However, there is some confusion about exactly where these famous tablets of law were delivered to Moses on the mountain-top. The mountain that Moses ascended to receive them has two names, or it is two different mountains. 'Horeb' in Deuteronomy and 'Sinai' in Exodus could be the same place or different places in close proximity. The different names are usually attributed to the likelihood that two accounts of the same event were written by different people, so most scholars believe that Sinai and Horeb are the same mountain. Even so, although a modern part of the Middle East bears the name 'the Sinai Peninsula', this is not necessarily the location of Moses' Mount Sinai.

The Jewish historian Josephus identified Sinai as a mountain between Egypt and Arabia, being of great height with sharp precipices. There are actually three major peaks in that region—Jebel Musa, Mount Catherine and Ras Safsafa. Many pilgrims visit St Catherine's Monastery at the base of Mount Catherine and are encouraged to consider themselves as being at or near the place where Moses received the tablets of the law. It is worth remembering, though, that Josephus did not know any of these peaks as Sinai, and the region is called Sinai only because Christian tradition locates these events there. Local tradition in the Sinai Peninsula locates Moses' peak on the nearby Jebel Musa, but it could be somewhere completely different. Suggestions include locations further east, into modern Jordan or even Saudi Arabia. The wonderful tourist site of Petra, home of the Nabateans, is sometimes claimed to be the site of Sinai/Horeb—specifically, the Mount of the Altar, an intrepid but accessible climb to this day. This is not such a far-fetched suggestion, for the valley in which Petra's amazing carved tombs are found is 'Wadi Musa' (Valley of Moses), and not far away is 'Ain Musa', a location claimed to be the place known as Meribah, where Moses struck the rock and water gushed forth (see Exodus 17:1–7).

Complex as it is to locate Sinai/Horeb accurately, the

enterprise can distract us from the significance, in world history and culture, of the giving of the law. We often take the ten commandments for granted, and a cursory glance at the news media reveals that they are often broken or ignored. Idolatry, murder, adultery, theft, secularism, blasphemy and perjury are commonplace, and the idea of keeping one day a week 'holy' or as a day of rest has been much undermined in recent years. It is not long since Sunday trading was still forbidden; those who tried to keep it so argued that the sabbath was not simply a divine encouragement to rest and pray, but also fulfilled the psychological and social need for a day when a family might do something as simple as eat together at the same table at the same time. Making sure everyone has a day off is not the same thing as making sure they can spend it with loved ones or friends.

Many people are offended when God's name is trivialised or made an exclamation of mild surprise, horror or inconvenience. The phrase 'O God' begins our communal prayers, but it is also what many people exclaim when someone says or does something annoying or upsetting. Abbreviated to 'OMG', insult is added to injury—abbreviation added to misuse. Nowadays the Lord's name is taken in vain routinely, yet Moses' original community dared not even utter the name of the Lord, but used only the first syllable, 'Yah' (as in 'Yahweh'). The modern trivialisation of divinity is not only a symptom of disregard for the traditions of faith and the reality of God, it is also a breach of the third commandment.

Idolatry was rife among neighbouring communities in Moses' day. Indeed, much of the Jewish law was a response and reaction to the customs of the surrounding lands and tribes, ensuring that the Hebrew law (Torah) would mark out the Israelites as worshippers of their one God. There are still cultures today that venerate statues, and Christianity has faced controversies in the past over the use of icons or statues of saints in worship. Idolatry is not simply about statues and graven images, but concerns anything that becomes an object of devotion or obsession. Current idolatrous attitudes to wealth, possessions, status, power, influence or comfort are so endemic in society that we generally both accept and overlook them. Censure of covetousness, greed, self-importance or ambition is now unthinkable in a culture that rests upon them. Similarly, the obsessive behaviour and desire to emulate others that we find in people of all ages, with regard to sporting heroes, celebrities, politicians and peer groups, is the oxygen for the individualistic bloodstream that flows through the beating heart of tolerant indifference pervading modern life. We accept everything but care about very little, and the graven images we set up to worship now are not even false gods; they are ourselves.

The commandment to honour one's parents may seem to go without saying, and, like many of the commandments, has its root in the need for good and proper relationships within the community. Jesus' own summary of the law, 'Love the Lord your God... [and] love your neighbour as yourself' (Mark 12:30–31) reminds us that we are called to be in a right relationship with God and with each other. The ten commandments point us towards achieving that aim.

Murder, theft and perjury (giving false witness) are still crimes in most societies and are widely recognised as wrong, sometimes alongside adultery. Wrong or illegal they may still be, but they are widely encountered and are even seen as justified in some contexts.

The ten commandments are a time capsule of ancient values. They reflect their own age but still prick our consciences today. They reflect stability amid constant change and remain at the foundations of many cultures. When we examine them, they reveal the ancient culture on which our own is founded, but they also hold a mirror to our own. In either case, their creation and their survival are proof that we have always needed commandments, still do and always shall.

I'll read the histories of thy love,
And keep thy laws in sight,
While through thy promises I rove
With ever fresh delight.
ISAAC WATTS (1674–1748)

1 January

Sin comes into the world

The woman said to the serpent, 'We may eat of the fruit of the trees in the garden; but God said, "You shall not eat of the fruit of the tree that is in the middle of the garden, nor shall you touch it, or you shall die."' But the serpent said to the woman, 'You will not die; for God knows that when you eat of it your eyes will be opened, and you will be like God, knowing good and evil.' So when the woman saw that the tree was good for food, and that it was a delight to the eyes, and that the tree was to be desired to make one wise, she took of its fruit and ate; and she also gave some to her husband, who was with her, and he ate. Then the eyes of both were opened, and they knew that they were naked; and they sewed fig leaves together and made loincloths for themselves.

They heard the sound of the Lord God walking in the garden at the time of the evening breeze, and the man and his wife hid themselves from the presence of the Lord God among the trees of the garden. But the Lord God called to the man, and said to him, 'Where are you?' He said, 'I heard the sound of you in the garden, and I was afraid, because I was naked; and I hid myself.' He said, 'Who told you that you were naked? Have you eaten from the tree of which I commanded you not to eat?' The man said, 'The woman whom you gave to be with me, she gave me fruit from the tree, and I ate.' Then the Lord God said to the woman, 'What is this that you have done?' The woman said, 'The serpent tricked me, and I ate'.

GENESIS 3:2–13

This is an earthshaking moment in human history and culture. Whether or not Adam and Eve were 'real' people, sin is real; we only have to look around us to see that. It is also clear that, from the very beginning of recorded history, sin involved transgressing the laws not of humankind but of God. Adam and Eve's sin was to disobey God, their creator, sustainer and, ultimately, in Christ, their redeemer.

This story has even more to say to us than it did perhaps a century or two ago. Our inability to take responsibility for our actions, along with our tendency to find excuses, scapegoats or others to blame, is as rife in the boardroom and political chamber as it is in the playground or bedroom. Whatever happens, it is always someone else's fault, and to admit guilt is to admit failure and lose face. The media do not help, constantly looking for foibles and falsehoods, for we belong to a nation that loves a good scandal.

The story is set in the garden of Eden. Eden, we are told, is a very lovely place, a paradise of flowing water and plant life, and God places Adam in it to till and care for it. Humanity was created to look after the earth: it is, to a great extent, our job, our God-given task. Soon Eve is created to share in this responsibility, and, just as Adam is invited to name everything, Eve is to be known as the mother of all living things (Genesis 3:20). Mythical and mysterious these ideas may all appear to be, but underlying them is a key human role and duty, to God and the environment.

Millennia later, we find ourselves on a planet that our intellect has enabled us to understand. We sit on a 4.5 billion-year-old planet that is small but quite possibly unique in the cosmos, which will probably lose all of its water in about a billion years' time and thus be rendered inhospitable to life. Yet we have also discovered that there are various ways in which our own activities could render earth uninhabitable long before then. We consume the world's resources, poison and overpopulate land and sea, develop horrendous weapons and a mentality to use them, and cause countless species to disappear. On the other hand, we have great skills of insight and wisdom; we are able to look into the past and the future in order to learn from what has happened and predict what could or will happen. We can predict earthquakes, tsunamis and volcanic eruptions—at least sometimes. In this we are unique: we can look forwards and backwards at the comings and goings of life, and act, or fail to act, accordingly. We do not have to believe in Adam and Eve to do this, or to recognise the wrongs that are perpetrated against the peoples and animals of our planet by those who do not care, who want to make money or who choose to disbelieve the findings of science. Meanwhile, some others blame it all on God, or even take the view that the effect we have on the destiny of earth is somehow part of God's plan.

Many people do not see the hand of God in any of this or, indeed, in anything at all; they dismiss Adam and Eve as mythical fairytale characters created for a naïve worldview, which has been superseded by science and philosophy. Yet many who despise or deny divinity recognise that we have a problem with global warming (for example) and that it is, in some sense, our fault. Impending ecological catastrophe is a kind of secular sin, and, as we approach the 'tipping point', beyond which no reversal of the spiralling trend towards disaster is possible, we hear stronger accusations of blame and a greater emphasis on what we may or may not be able to do about it. In secular terms, we have sinned, and the only people who can get us out of it, the only people who can save us, are us.

So it has come to pass that we have abandoned God while tending his garden, claiming it for ourselves, messing it up and failing to steward it wisely; and we think we can save ourselves from ourselves, by using the same intellect and wisdom we have always used. Such intellect and wisdom, it might be said, is plucked straight from the tree of the knowledge of good and evil. We have never fully learned to tell the difference between them, and you can't have one without the other. This is why we cannot save ourselves from our own sins and why we need a second Adam, Jesus Christ, to show us the way to a new creation and a new discipleship, which depends on God rather than ourselves.

O loving wisdom of our God!
When all was sin and shame,
a second Adam to the fight
and to the rescue came.

O wisest love! that flesh and blood,
which did in Adam fail,
should strive afresh against the foe,
should strive, and should prevail.

JOHN HENRY NEWMAN (1801–90)

2 January

Arriving at the beginning

In the beginning when God created the heavens and the earth, the earth was a formless void and darkness covered the face of the deep, while a wind from God swept over the face of the waters. Then God said, 'Let there be light'; and there was light. And God saw that the light was good; and God separated the light from the darkness. God called the light Day, and the darkness he called Night. And there was evening and there was morning, the first day... And God said, 'Let there be a dome in the midst of the waters, and let it separate the waters from the waters... Let the waters under the sky be gathered together into one place, and let the dry land appear.'... The earth brought forth vegetation: plants yielding seed of every kind, and trees of every kind bearing fruit with the seed in it... And God said, 'Let there be lights in the dome of the sky to separate the day from the night; and let them be for signs and for seasons and for days and years... Let the waters bring forth swarms of living creatures, and let birds fly above the earth across the dome of the sky... Let the earth bring forth living creatures of every kind: cattle and creeping things and wild animals of the earth of every kind... Let us make humankind in our image, according to our likeness.'

GENESIS 1:1–6, 9, 12, 14, 20, 24, 26

We have reached the end of our journey through time and space. Now we arrive at the beginning of the Bible, where those ancient and beautiful opening words attempt to explain who we are and how we came to be. Modern scholarship tells us that there were at least five writers of the Pentateuch (the first five books of the Old Testament), and that is why there are, in fact, two different accounts of creation in Genesis, in chapters 1 and 2. These accounts should be seen not as contradictory but as complementary. Similarly, it is more helpful to see the discoveries of modern science as complementary than contradictory to biblical accounts. Whether we think in terms of six days of creation or the Big Bang theory, we can be inspired and enlightened, by so many zones of enquiry and knowledge, about the human condition, the universe and our place within it. It is perfectly possible to hold these things together, intellectually and spiritually.

Professor Stephen Hawking disagrees:

Because there is a law such as gravity, the universe can and will create itself from nothing. Spontaneous creation is the reason there is something rather than nothing, why the Universe exists, why we exist. It is not necessary to invoke God to light the blue touch paper and set the Universe going.

'EUREKA', *THE TIMES*, 2 SEPTEMBER 2010, P. 25

For Hawking and others, God is unnecessary. All the universe needs is a set of equations, probabilities and coincidences that lead to our current situation. If, as Hawking and others believe, we live in the midst of a multiverse (a vast collection of universes), then everything and anything that *can* happen *has* happened, somewhere, sometime. Because there are so many universes, it can, will and even *did* happen without the need for any non-physical force to be involved. Hawking takes 'God' to be such a non-physical force, and so inevitably rules him out of the equation.

There are at least three possibilities for how the universe came into existence. We inhabit a planet that is distinctively set up not only to bring about carbon-based life (that's us), but to sustain it. Tweak gravity, or the distance of the earth from the sun, by only a small amount, and we could not exist. The sun is 400 times the size of the moon, and the sun is 400 times further away from us than the moon, which means that it is possible for the moon to completely eclipse the sun, as we sometimes witness here on earth. We may say that this is all just a coincidence, an unnecessary fluke. This is one of the three possibilities—that chance, not providence, brings things into being.

A second possibility is that there is a Creator who made it so. Given the near impossibility of meeting each and every one of the millions of criteria that needed to be met, if our planet was to be even vaguely interesting, let alone as glorious as it is, many people feel that divinity is the best near-explanation we have. They don't *need* this explanation; they don't simply *feel* it; nor do they read it and take it at face value from an old book, combined with a few legends and scriptures. No, they think about it long and hard.

The third option is M-theory and the idea of the multiverse. It is a philosopher's old chestnut, on which Hawking puts some flesh. It is sometimes said that if you put enough monkeys in a room for long enough and provide them with typewriters, they will eventually come up with the complete works of Shakespeare. This is partly a joke about probability theory and the vastness of space and time: anything can happen, given enough time and space. The multiverse theory of the universe is like the monkeys and the typewriters. Multiverse theory says that if you allocate enough time and space, through multiple universes, some of which exist in dimensions we cannot perceive, then somewhere and sometime our distinctive circumstances will recur. It can happen again because it already has happened, and the vast opportunity presented by a multiverse for it to do so means that it has done or will do. So, if something is probable or possible, it is inevitable. Somewhere out there is another planet, not dissimilar to ours, where life has evolved. This is why Stephen Hawking believes in extraterrestrial life.

M-theory is basically mathematical and no individual takes credit for it. Hawking himself admits that it may not be possible to decipher it, and no one has adequately defined what it really is. Hawking and others believe that M-theory has the answers but admit that there is a lot of work to be done. It is a theory that demands a degree of imagination or faith. Yet even if it could be proved that there is a collection of universes we might call a multiverse, and even if it could still be said that we don't *need* God to set it going, none of this has any bearing on our own personal encounters with Jesus Christ through the Holy Spirit of God our creator.

We do not need God to be necessary; we only need him to be real, which is quite another matter. And God *is* real—in the breaking of day, the breaking of bread and the breaking of our hearts when loved ones die. God is real to us in the creative outpourings of musicians, artists, poets and preachers who inspire and move us. God is real, here and now, in the fibres of our being and in the furthest outreaches of the cosmos. And that's why the questions about whether there is one universe or a zillion universes in a multiverse, or whether God is necessary for creation or not, are simply academic.

Science explores your reason's ways
And faith can this impart,
That in the face of Christ, our gaze
Looks deep within your heart.
ALBERT FREDERICK BAYLY (1901–84)

3 January

Genealogy (Matthew)

An account of the genealogy of Jesus the Messiah, the son of David, the son of Abraham.

Abraham was the father of Isaac, and Isaac the father of Jacob, and Jacob the father of Judah and his brothers, and Judah the father of Perez and Zerah by Tamar, and Perez the father of Hezron, and Hezron the father of Aram, and Aram the father of Aminadab, and Aminadab the father of Nahshon, and Nahshon the father of Salmon, and Salmon the father of Boaz by Rahab, and Boaz the father of Obed by Ruth, and Obed the father of Jesse, and Jesse the father of King David.

And David was the father of Solomon by the wife of Uriah, and Solomon the father of Rehoboam, and Rehoboam the father of Abijah, and Abijah the father of Asaph, and Asaph the father of Jehoshaphat, and Jehoshaphat the father of Joram, and Joram the father of Uzziah, and Uzziah the father of Jotham, and Jotham the father of Ahaz, and Ahaz the father of Hezekiah, and Hezekiah the father of Manasseh, and Manasseh the father of Amos, and Amos the father of Josiah, and Josiah the father of Jechoniah and his brothers, at the time of the deportation to Babylon.

And after the deportation to Babylon: Jechoniah was the father of Salathiel, and Salathiel the father of Zerubbabel, and Zerubbabel the father of Abiud, and Abiud the father of Eliakim, and Eliakim the father of Azor, and Azor the father of Zadok, and Zadok the father of Achim, and Achim the father of Eliud, and Eliud the father of Eleazar, and Eleazar the father of Matthan, and Matthan the father of Jacob, and Jacob the father of Joseph the husband of Mary, of whom Jesus was born, who is called the Messiah.

So all the generations from Abraham to David are fourteen generations; and from David to the deportation to Babylon, fourteen generations; and from the deportation to Babylon to the Messiah, fourteen generations.

MATTHEW 1:1–17

Have you studied your family tree? With TV programmes asking celebrities who they think they are, and much census data being made available online these days, a trend has developed to 'do the family history'. Previous generations had a family Bible passed down the line, in which births, marriages and deaths were recorded. In this way people grew up knowing who their immediate forebears were—who was related to whom, and on which side of the family each member was. Because there wasn't much technology to assist, they would have found it hard to do research, but, on the other hand, they had access to their story passed down through word of mouth and scraps of paper.

Travel back two millennia and we find that Gospel writer Matthew was writing for those who also had a sense of their place in history: this is why he made the unique effort to draw Jesus' family tree in such detail. His readers knew the people in his list far better than we do now, and the connections among them that Matthew itemised would have been impressive. That Jesus was descended from Abraham and David was of great importance to the Jews for whom Matthew was writing.

Abraham is still revered by Christians, Jews and Muslims

alike, all of whom treat him as the father of a line of later leaders and prophets. Sadly, this can be a cause of division, even though Matthew was trying to unite the people of faith along a timeline of universal salvation. We must not forget Abraham, our common ancestor of faith.

Yet there is sin in this list. There is sin everywhere, even among those whom we revere as great religious leaders. Matthew wants to connect Jesus to a list of spiritual heroes, but they were sinners too, like you and me. David infamously committed adultery with Bathsheba, the wife of Uriah the Hittite, whom David caused to be killed in battle (see 2 Samuel 11), and his son Solomon, although blessed with wisdom, was not without his faults (see 1 Kings 11). Solomon's son Rehoboam also forsook the law of the Lord (2 Chronicles 12:1), and so it continues down the line until we reach the man at the head of the list, Jesus. Although he is without sin, the others, like every human being before or since, had weaknesses and flaws. This connects them, and Jesus, to you and me. We all stand in that great line of sinful, saved humanity.

Matthew's all-too-human list takes us on to a period of judgement. Jeremiah, Ezekiel and others saw the deportation, or exile, of the Jews to Babylon as a just punishment for abandoning the ways of God. Matthew mentions the exile specifically (v. 11), and it marks a useful historical pausing point. It also reminds us of the road from perdition on which Jesus leads us, for Matthew carries on through sin until he reaches Jesus, who, because he himself is divine and sinless, clears sin away by his death and turns us all around, pointing us in a new direction and sending us out on the road to salvation.

From Matthew we get not only a sense of Jesus' place in history, but also a sense of the pace of history. Forty-two generations are listed, and Matthew suggests that it was not really a very long time between Abraham and Christ. In this way, Abraham is brought closer to Jesus' generation, and Jesus is similarly made real even to us: we need to go back only 33 60-year lifetimes to meet Christ. Seen in this light, the events of the Bible are much closer to us than we might have realised. By reminding his readers of the relatively recent history preceding the birth of Christ, Matthew brings that world nearer in time; and, reading it now, we are reminded that we are closer in time to Matthew than he was to Abraham.

Amid all these comings and goings, we recognise that Jesus is not simply a figure of the past, a historical figure whose wanderings in Palestine are obscured by desert dust and the passage of progressively more enlightened time. Matthew brought Jesus into focus for his own generation. Since then, many people have distanced Jesus from the real issues and needs of his and our own time. It is good to look down the road that leads directly from Christ to our day and contemplate the people, events and ideologies that have affected faith over the years. Church history is not always pleasant to contemplate, and there is much in it to lament, but through it all we can trace a direct line to Jesus and his early followers, just as Matthew was able to connect Jesus to those who drew their inspiration and their bloodline from Abraham. In the great scheme of things, it was all quite recent.

The whole triumphant host give thanks to God on high;
'Hail, Father, Son, and Holy Ghost,' they ever cry.
Hail, Abraham's God, and mine! (I join the heav'nly lays,)
All might and majesty are Thine, and endless praise.

FROM THE YIGDAL OF DANIEL BEN JUDAH, C.1400, PARAPHRASED BY
THOMAS OLIVERS (1725–99)

4 January

The beginning of the Gospel (Mark)

The beginning of the good news of Jesus Christ, the Son of God. As it is written in the prophet Isaiah, 'See, I am sending my messenger ahead of you, who will prepare your way; the voice of one crying out in the wilderness: "Prepare the way of the Lord, make his paths straight!"' John the baptiser appeared in the wilderness, proclaiming a baptism of repentance for the forgiveness of sins. And people from the whole Judean countryside and all the people of Jerusalem were going out to him, and were baptised by him in the river Jordan, confessing their sins. Now John was clothed with camel's hair, with a leather belt around his waist, and he ate locusts and wild honey. He proclaimed, 'The one who is more powerful than I is coming after me; I am not worthy to stoop down and untie the thong of his sandals. I have baptised you with water; but he will baptise you with the Holy Spirit.'

MARK 1:1–8

Today we are at the beginning of Mark's Gospel, the first Gospel to be written: 'The beginning of the good news of Jesus Christ, the Son of God.' The sound is staccato— 'Bang! Bang!'—because here at the beginning everything is compacted, rather like the literary equivalent of the Big Bang. Way back in the history of the universe, everything was contained in an infinitesimally small speck of space and time. Then, incredibly fast and furiously, everything—

literally everything—exploded and expanded outwards. A metaphorically equivalent kind of thing happens in this, the Big Bang of the New Testament. From these first words of the first chapter of the first Gospel to be written emerges everything—not just the story of Jesus' birth, life, ministry, death and resurrection, but the very meaning of it all. Mark wrote, 'The beginning of the good news of Jesus Christ, the Son of God.' That's *it*. The blue touchpaper is lit. The beginning is both the opening bang and the summary of the whole thing. As an opening sentence, it is unparalleled in all literature.

But of what is it a summary? Or rather, of what is it the beginning? If we turn to the very last words of Mark's Gospel, 16 chapters later, we find that it doesn't really end. Rather, Mark describes an ongoing process of the birth and growth of the fledgling church: 'And they went out and proclaimed the good news everywhere, while the Lord worked with them and confirmed the message by the signs that accompanied it' (16:20). Everything in between the beginning and the end is an account both conflated from the 33 years of Jesus' life and expanded from the word 'gospel'. Rather like the creation of the universe, it all escalates from there.

So what is this 'gospel' or 'good news' of Jesus Christ? The Greek word is *evangelion*, and, in the context of the Roman rule of Jewish territories in the first century, it was proclaimed as the 'good news', usually, of a victory in battle. The good news meant, 'We won!' This idea features in accounts of the lives and achievements of the Roman emperors, who were honoured in their day as gods in their own right. So, concealed in the concept of the word 'gospel' is the idea of victory—victory for a god. We might also be reminded of Paul's Easter words: '"Death has been swallowed up in victory." "Where, O death, is your victory? Where, O death, is your sting?" The sting of death is sin, and the power of sin is the law. But thanks be to God, who gives us the victory through our Lord Jesus Christ' (1 Corinthians 15:54–57).

Mark is not just aping the Roman militaristic victory cry; he is also drawing on a tradition from Isaiah, the prophet who is most associated with prophecies concerning Jesus, for the concept of *evangelion* was not limited to the military and political sphere. In Isaiah, 'good news' refers to God's salvation, when peace and release from oppression will 'rain down righteousness' (Isaiah 45:8). As Mark goes on to say, quoting Isaiah 40:3, the beginning of the beginning is revealed in the sending of a messenger, who turns out to be John the Baptist. He is the last of the prophets and the forerunner of Christ, the pivot on which the old becomes the new. His task is to herald the beginning of the good news of the victory of Jesus Christ, the Son of God.

Mark's use of 'Christ' as a kind of surname reveals an intentional meaning, for he is also telling us succinctly that this Jesus of Nazareth—yes, *him*, the one who was crucified and rose again—was, in fact, the Christ, and we take this for granted in the simple act of naming or referring to him. He is not just Jesus, the Son of God; he is Jesus *Christ*, the Son of God.

This might well have sounded strangely radical to Mark's readers and hearers. Any Greek (the Gospel was, of course, written in Greek) would have assumed that Mark was referring to someone like one of their mythological children of the gods. Being the son of *a* god was special, but it was not unheard of. For example, Heracles (Hercules) was the son of the god Zeus and his human mother Alcmene. But Mark was saying that Jesus was not *a* son of *a* god, but *the* Son of *the* God. Underneath was the implication that there is, was and only ever could be one God.

Meanwhile, Jews, reading or hearing Mark's opening gambit, would have thought that he was referring to Jesus as some kind of king. In Psalm 2:6–7, the psalmist wrote, '"I have set my king on Zion, my holy hill." I will tell of the decree of the Lord: He said to me, "You are my son; today I have begotten you."' This idea is also picked up in the letter to the Hebrews (1:5–9). If we pile all this together, we get, at the kernel of Mark's opening line, the idea that this is the beginning of the coming of Jesus the Messiah, king of the nations and Son of the one God, whose victory over oppression, sin and death will unfold from all that follows.

The opening phrase of Mark's Gospel carries us right through everything that follows. As T.S. Eliot put it, in words that are engraved on his memorial plaque in East Coker Church, Somerset, placed there on Easter Day 1965, 'In my beginning is my end, in my end is my beginning.' In this opening verse is the full circle of meaning, as the gospel, the good news, is begun, continued and lifted beyond the confines of history. In 'Here begins the good news of Jesus Christ, the Son of God' is the beginning and the end of everything we need to know, believe and live out in our lives.

Hark, a herald voice is sounding:
'Christ is nigh,' it seems to say.
Cast away the dreams of darkness,
O ye children of the day!
LATIN, TENTH CENTURY, TRANS. EDWARD CASWALL (1814–78)

Making history (Luke)

Since many have undertaken to set down an orderly account of the events that have been fulfilled among us, just as they were handed on to us by those who from the beginning were eyewitnesses and servants of the word, I too decided, after investigating everything carefully from the very first, to write an orderly account for you, most excellent Theophilus, so that you may know the truth concerning the things about which you have been instructed.

LUKE 1:1–4

This passage, which precedes the birth narratives of John the Baptist and then Jesus, is often overlooked, being seen as a mere preamble to the accounts that unfold. Luke, traditionally reckoned to have been a physician from Antioch, sets out his stall as one historian among many. As we read his opening lines, we notice that he begins by stating that others have written accounts of the life and ministry of Jesus. He also tells us that there have been eyewitnesses to the events he will describe, and that some of these people were 'servants of the word', using the same Greek word (*logos*) that John does in the opening of his Gospel. Luke's motivation here is to offer his own version of events, in response to the efforts that have been made by others. He is sending it to Theophilus, who may or may not have been a real, individual person. Some scholars argue that Theophilus, which means 'friend of God', is a generic name and that Luke might be using something similar to the Victorian novelists' convention of addressing the person reading a book as 'gentle reader'. Any author writing anything (myself included!) imagines people reading what is being written, and writes for them. Gentle reader of *this* book, I put it to you that Luke may have had a real person called Theophilus in mind, or he may not, in which case he was simply addressing himself to you and me.

If Theophilus was a real person, he could have been a Roman official (who might even have asked Luke to write the Gospel), and the fact that Luke calls him 'excellent Theophilus' points to this possibility. Not only is Luke respectful, but he is being respectful in a conventional way. Some scholars have even gone as far as to name the official, believing that he might have been Titus Flavius Sabinus II, who died in the year 69 and was the older brother of the man who became Emperor Vespasian. The Coptic Church of Egypt believes that Theophilus was a Jew living in Alexandria, and another suggestion is that Theophilus was a lawyer who represented the apostle Paul in Rome. There is also a theory that Luke's target was Theophilus ben Ananus, who was a Sadducee and high priest in the temple from AD37 to 41. Yet another contender is Mattathias ben Theophilus, who was high priest from 65 to 66.

It is appropriate to apply this historical detail to Luke's writing, because it is what he set out to do himself. Whoever Theophilus was, it was clearly Luke's purpose, expressed at the outset, to order the oral and written accounts already in circulation and set down an account that would be an honest witness to the good news that was arousing such interest and attention. Thus Luke set himself up as an historian of discernment, who used primary and secondary sources to record what had happened, in order to determine what would happen in future.

This is what history does. History is not simply about the past; it is concerned very much with the future. In the comings and goings it records, it not only tells us what happened but also determines what will be deemed significant in the future. Napoleon Bonaparte famously and ironically declared, 'History is written by the winners', and he was not wrong. To some extent, Luke is seeking to 'win' with his account for Theophilus—to win him over, and to win over you and me, so that we might believe and trust in the good news of Jesus Christ. He does this by taking on the other accounts to which he makes veiled reference, correcting, replacing and authenticating them in the process. Luke was also the author of Acts, which opens in a similar way, establishing itself as the sequel to the Gospel: 'In the first book, Theophilus, I wrote about all that Jesus did and taught from the beginning until the day when he was taken up to heaven, after giving instructions through the Holy Spirit to the apostles whom he had chosen' (Acts 1:1–2).

At the opening of his Gospel, Luke stresses that he is trying to bring 'order' to the plethora of stories concerning the life, death and resurrection of Jesus. Whoever Theophilus was, Luke believed that he would want an orderly account, and Luke does proceed in an orderly fashion—more orderly than Mark and John, for sure, both of whom start not at the beginning but with John the Baptist. Matthew, as we have seen, begins with Jesus' genealogy and launches into birth narratives that focus on Joseph and the magi. Luke starts with the birth of John the Baptist, so that the angel's annunciation to Mary can be put into context. Luke is also the only writer to tell us anything about Jesus' childhood.

More significantly, Luke carries the story beyond the resurrection of Jesus, unlike the other three, who stop there. In Acts, he takes us through the growth of the early church and, most specifically, describes the ministry of Paul. Acts closes with Paul in Rome, with no hint of his execution to come. Luke–Acts, then, carries us from Zechariah in the temple through to Paul, framing Jesus in a historical context, with the resurrection effectively at the centre of its historical view.

Luke's historical scope is vast; like a great novelist, he brings us up to his central character and then leads us beyond him to consider the impact of his deeds and words. George Eliot and D.H. Lawrence were masters of this approach: in novels such as *Middlemarch*, *The Mill on the Floss*, *Sons and Lovers* and *Women in Love* the central characters are cast in the context of their ancestors and descendants. It is a magisterial way of helping readers to understand the bigger picture, in order to absorb not only the history but also the future significance of the events described and the meaning of the creative plan underpinning the whole. This is what Luke does for us, and it makes him one of the greatest writers of historical literature that the world has known—fittingly, for Luke's words point us to Jesus Christ, the only Word the world has known.

Loved physician! For his word,
Lo, the gospel page burns brighter,
Mission servant of the Lord,
Painter true, and perfect writer;
Saviour, of thy bounty send
Such as Luke of gospel story,
Friends to all in body's prison
Till the sufferers see thy glory.
HARDWICKE DRUMMOND RAWNSLEY (1851–1920)

6 January

Conclusion:
'In the beginning' (John)

In the beginning was the Word, and the Word was with God, and the Word was God. The same was in the beginning with God. All things were made by him; and without him was not any thing made that was made. In him was life; and the life was the light of men. And the light shineth in darkness; and the darkness comprehended it not.

There was a man sent from God, whose name was John. The same came for a witness, to bear witness of the Light, that all men through him might believe. He was not that Light, but was sent to bear witness of that Light. That was the true Light, which lighteth every man that cometh into the world. He was in the world, and the world was made by him, and the world knew him not. He came unto his own, and his own received him not. But as many as received him, to them gave he power to become the sons of God, even to them that believe on his name: Which were born, not of blood, nor of the will of the flesh, nor of the will of man, but of God. And the Word was made flesh, and dwelt among us, (and we beheld his glory, the glory as of the only begotten of the Father,) full of grace and truth.

JOHN 1:1–14 (KJV)

Now we have finally arrived at the beginning. We end with the opening words of the last Gospel. For many of us, this is the supreme text of the Bible, usually read from the King James Bible as the climax of the 'Service of Nine Lessons and Carols'. It is the pinnacle of the story of salvation, yet it throws its roots into the beginning of time and sums up the meaning and purpose of the coming of Christ. It carries us back to the beginning of all things, to the Big Bang of creation itself, and locates God in Christ at the epicentre of everything.

It was Edward Benson (1829–96) who thought of placing 'In the beginning was the Word' at the end of a carol service. He was a schoolmaster at Rugby School, then Headmaster of Wellington School, and became Chancellor of Lincoln Cathedral in 1872 before being appointed the first Bishop of Truro in 1877. He became Archbishop of Canterbury in 1883. While in Truro, he devised a liturgy for Christmas Eve which he called 'The Festival of Nine Lessons', and it was first used in Truro Cathedral on Christmas Eve 1880. The famous tradition is that Truro Cathedral was little more than a wooden structure at the time, and, by scheduling the service for 10.00 pm, he hoped to keep the men out of the pubs. It was another 38 years before the organist of King's College, Cambridge, Arthur Henry Mann, took up the idea, guided by the Dean of Chapel, Eric Milner-White. On Christmas Eve 1918, with World War I recently ended, a new tradition was born, which survives in many places: the story of redemption is read through, beginning with Adam and Eve (read by a child) and continuing to the visit of the magi, culminating with a senior cleric reading from the first chapter of John's Gospel, with the congregation standing.

The description of a light shining in the midst of uncomprehending darkness is so familiar that we may forget how radical and striking it is. Without light we can see nothing;

we *are* nothing; we cannot survive. For someone who had never encountered light at all, it would be unimaginable, impossible to comprehend. So when a light appeared, the reaction would be not, 'Ah, someone switched the light on' but, rather, 'What is *that*?' The nearest any human could come to this kind of experience would be if someone born totally blind were very suddenly enabled to see. However, stories we hear today of the blind being given sight, through science, invariably involve the restoration of sight that has been lost through disease or accident, rather than sight given to someone who has never seen in their life. So the words with which John begins his Gospel describe a phenomenon that we cannot imagine—light in a context where no one understands what light is.

In the first chapter of Genesis, we hear that the first thing God created was light. This means that there was no one in existence to understand what light was—and, as John puts it, referring to the same event, not even the darkness could understand or conceive what light might be. In creating light, God, who had never done anything before, did a new thing, setting in motion a process of creation, redemption and sustenance that brings you to the very moment of reading this book, and beyond. The timeline is endless and, inasmuch as we cannot measure it, without a beginning.

John, having taken us back towards that incomprehensible beginning of all things, introduces the character of John the Baptist, a man of whom his readers would have heard, who was very much real flesh and blood to them. So, the incomprehensible is connected to the real fleshly presence not only of John but of Jesus, who, John has just told us, is in fact that very light. Jesus is the incomprehensible light shining in the darkness, but he is also the man who walks among us, uniting the divine and the human and connecting the temporal with the eternal. In Christ, God submitted himself to the boundaries of linear human time only briefly, and he did so to reveal his eternal presence as Alpha and Omega, the beginning and the end. Jesus' coming was incomprehensible to those in the world who did not know and would not receive him. Christ coming to the world is like light coming to a world that knows only darkness. Yet some did recognise and follow, and that calling was and is truly a great and gracious gift of God.

John 1 is one of the most beautiful yet most opaque passages in the New Testament. Its language and meaning are mysterious in their profundity. We are carried to the very beginning of time and then brought back to what was the present moment for John, the moment of incarnation when God, the utterer of the word of creation, became human. This is a staggering truth, on which the whole of our Christian faith rests. Whether we are coming or going, it is the journey from creation, through incarnation, ministry, passion, death, resurrection and ascension, that brings us into the Church of Christ, created at Pentecost, nurtured by God's Spirit, and destined for eternal resurrection life. It is on this inspiring journey of hope that we are borne onward and upward in every time and place, then, now and always.

Word supreme, before creation
born of God eternally,
who didst will for our salvation
to be born on earth, and die;
well thy saints have kept their station,
watching till thine hour is nigh.
JOHN KEBLE (1792–1866)

Discussion topics for groups

At the end of each chapter of this book, there is a verse from a hymn, reflecting the Bible reading and the meditation upon it. Individuals or groups, reading alone or together, might like to sing or reflect on the hymn further. Another task, which may not be so easy, is to identify the hymns from which the verses are taken: some will be more familiar than others.

Here is a series of questions and thoughts for group discussion and reflection. In Lent, many church groups read a book and meet to discuss it. BRF has been promoting this approach, and publishing books with this noble goal in mind, for many years now. As a parish priest, though, I am all too well aware of the difficulties for group meetings as the rush towards Christmas accelerates, and as not only shopping and parties but carol services, mission activities and charity events pile up. Rather than divide the discussion questions into four weekly 'sessions', therefore, I offer them as a three-part list, in the hope that a group leader will be able to select, weight or balance them as it seems appropriate or useful. One suggestion might be to meet for a couple of weeks in Advent and reconvene in the new year. The final group of questions assumes a complete reading of the book. The number of sessions needed will depend on the size and gregarious nature of the group.

Many readers will not be part of a group at all, and this list is also for them, perhaps giving some food for focused personal reflection.

Questions to think about in Advent as you travel into the book

- What does it mean to die?
- Are you afraid of death?
- Do you believe in heaven and/or hell?
- What is judgement?
- Does it matter what you, or anyone else, believes about death?
- Who or what are funerals for?
- What would you like your epitaph to be?
- What experiences do you have of the Holy Land?
- Do you have any preconceptions about it?
- Does having been there (or not) affect the way you read the Bible?
- Is there a solution to the difficulties the region still experiences?
- Where does Jesus Christ fit into our hopes for world peace and regional stability?
- What should the relationship between Christians, Jews and Muslims look like?

Questions to think about before or after Christmas, in the midst of reading

- When, in your opinion, does Advent finally give way to Christmas nowadays?
- What is the difference between Advent and Christmas?
- What makes a good carol service? (Have a look at www. eauk.org/culture/statistics/christmas-facts-and-quotes. cfm. Some of the poetry of T.S. Eliot—especially the *Four Quartets*—might also help group discussion.

- What should the church be doing about Christmas?
- How can we connect 'our' Christmas to the events of 2000 years ago?
- What is time, and what does it have to do with the holy Trinity?

Questions to think about after Epiphany, having completed the book

- Did you have a 'good' Christmas?
- What were you expecting from the season, and were your hopes and expectations met, by yourself, by others or by God?
- Was anything different or special?
- What would you lament or give thanks for?
- What did Christmas do to or for you this year?
- Where was God for you this Christmas?
- Does this book's approach (reading the story backwards) work? Does it help in any way? Try to articulate or share how or why, and any insights gained.
- How does the first coming of Jesus relate to his second coming?
- What does the idea of 'the end being in the beginning' mean to you?

ENJOYED READING THIS ADVENT BOOK?

Did you know BRF publishes a new Lent and Advent book each year? All our Lent and Advent books are designed with a daily printed Bible reading, comment and reflection. Some can be used in groups and contain questions which can be used in a study or reading group.

Previous Advent books have included:

Longing, Waiting, Believing, Rodney Holder
Real God in the Real World, Trystan Owain Hughes
Companions on the Bethlehem Road, Rachel Boulding
The Incredible Journey, Steve Brady

If you would like to be kept in touch with information about our forthcoming Lent or Advent books, please complete the coupon below.

✂ -

❑ Please keep me in touch by post with forthcoming Lent or Advent books
❑ Please email me with details about forthcoming Lent or Advent books

Email address: _____

Name _____

Address_____

_____

_____

Postcode_____

Telephone_____

Signature _____

Please send this completed form to:

Freepost RRLH-JCYA-SZX
BRF, 15 The Chambers,
Vineyard, Abingdon,
OX14 3FE, United Kingdom

Tel. 01865 319700
Fax. 01865 319701
Email: enquiries@brf.org.uk

www.brf.org.uk

For more information, visit our website at **www.brf.org.uk**

BRF's Lent book for 2016

Dust and Glory

Daily Bible readings from Ash Wednesday to Easter Day

David Runcorn

Lent is one of the three 40-day 'seasons' in the church's year, besides Advent and the period from Easter to Pentecost. The name itself, Lent, derives from an ancient word meaning 'spring' or 'long', referring to the time of year when days are beginning to lengthen and the world is turning from winter cold and dark to the warmth and promise of spring. During this time, the church calls us to a special period of prayer, self-examination and teaching—and this book has been written to accompany you through that period, a time of turning from winter to spring, from death to life.

In *Dust and Glory*, the questions are as important as the answers, and may call us to deep heart-searching. The goal is always to draw us to authentic faith; a way of living and believing that is real and vulnerable, strong in knowing its limits, rooted in joy and wonder, blessed with the healing and merciful presence of God. Such faith acknowledges both the dust of our mortality and the glory that keeps breaking in with unexpected life, hope and new beginnings.

ISBN 978 0 85746 357 9   £7.99
Available from your local Christian bookshop or direct from BRF: please visit www.brfonline.org.uk

Enjoyed

this book?

Write a review—we'd love to hear what you think.
Email: reviews@brf.org.uk

Keep up to date—receive details of our new books as they happen.
Sign up for email news and select your interest groups at:
www.brfonline.org.uk/findoutmore/

Follow us on Twitter @brfonline

By post—to receive new title information by post (UK only), complete
the form below and post to: BRF Mailing Lists, 15 The Chambers, Vineyard,
Abingdon, Oxfordshire, OX14 3FE

Your Details
Name _____
Address_____
_____
Town/City _____ Post Code _____
Email_____

Your Interest Groups (*Please tick as appropriate)

- ☐ Advent/Lent
- ☐ Bible Reading & Study
- ☐ Children's Books
- ☐ Discipleship
- ☐ Leadership

- ☐ Messy Church
- ☐ Pastoral
- ☐ Prayer & Spirituality
- ☐ Resources for Children's Church
- ☐ Resources for Schools

Support your local bookshop
Ask about their new title information schemes.